Cambridge Elements ≡

Elements in the Economics of Emerging Markets
edited by
Bruno S. Sergi
Harvard University

HARNESSING SOVEREIGN WEALTH FUNDS IN EMERGING ECONOMIES TOWARD SUSTAINABLE DEVELOPMENT

Mona Mostafa El-Sholkamy
Mohammed Bin Rashid School of Government

Mohammad Habibur Rahman
Mohammed Bin Rashid School of Government

CAMBRIDGE
UNIVERSITY PRESS

CAMBRIDGE
UNIVERSITY PRESS

University Printing House, Cambridge CB2 8BS, United Kingdom

One Liberty Plaza, 20th Floor, New York, NY 10006, USA

477 Williamstown Road, Port Melbourne, VIC 3207, Australia

314–321, 3rd Floor, Plot 3, Splendor Forum, Jasola District Centre,
New Delhi – 110025, India

103 Penang Road, #05–06/07, Visioncrest Commercial, Singapore 238467

Cambridge University Press is part of the University of Cambridge.

It furthers the University's mission by disseminating knowledge in the pursuit of
education, learning, and research at the highest international levels of excellence.

www.cambridge.org
Information on this title: www.cambridge.org/9781009198189
DOI: 10.1017/9781009198172

© Mona Mostafa El-Sholkamy and Mohammad Habibur Rahman 2022

First published 2022

A catalogue record for this publication is available from the British Library.

ISBN 978-1-009-19818-9 Paperback
ISSN 2631-8598 (online)
ISSN 2631-858X (print)

Harnessing Sovereign Wealth Funds in Emerging Economies toward Sustainable Development

Elements in the Economics of Emerging Markets

DOI: 10.1017/9781009198172
First published online: July 2022

Mona Mostafa El-Sholkamy
Mohammed Bin Rashid School of Government

Mohammad Habibur Rahman
Mohammed Bin Rashid School of Government

Author for correspondence: Mona Mostafa El-Sholkamy,
mona.mostafa@aucegypt.edu; mona.elsholkamy@mbrsg.ac.ae

Abstract: Sovereign Wealth Funds are government investment vehicles that have been present for decades. They are usually characterized by minimum information disclosure; however, this situation differed after worldwide events shed light on the role they possess to mitigate their downturns. The substantial economic influence they bring along due to their size and long-term impact has recently created an uproar of debate that eventually led to the ratification of the Santiago Principles. The Principles set the stage for governing SWFs' operations and grant them more clarity. They also contribute to a more stable environment for cross-border investment flows. With the importance of SWFs, emerging economies also rose as key institutional investors; only this time they called for harnessing their funds toward sustainable development investment strategies. Despite pressuring need to improve transparency and governance structures of SWFs in emerging markets (EMs), the former are regarded as promising means for achieving the sustainable development goals.

Keywords: sovereign wealth funds, sustainable development, emerging markets, investment strategy, fiscal policy

ISBNs: 9781009198189 (PB), 9781009198172 (OC)
ISSNs: 2631-8598 (online), 2631-858X (print)

Contents

1 Introduction

1.1 Executive Summary

This Element explores how sovereign wealth funds could be impactful instruments of sustainable development in emerging markets (EMs). SWFs are state-owned investment vehicles intended to pursue national objectives (Wurster & Schlosser, 2021). They also come with different mandates; some as developmental, others as stabilization and saving funds. They are cushioned on assets under their direct management (known as assets under management, AUM), and they seek to further accumulate those through an amalgamation of investment strategies. They have recently demonstrated modern outlooks to their investment portfolios and partnerships, where they deep dive into untraditional ventures with both private and public sector partners. They have risen from many countries around the world, but special interest is currently given to those from emerging economies and markets. As a powerful token in the hands of state owners, SWFs possess the ability to embark on untapped niches and achieve investment goals of a more sustainable nature. There is no doubt though that being state-owned enterprises, SWF investments are often accused of being used to advance certain political aims. Such accusations are notably connected with investments from strong EMs into much "weaker" ones, suggesting that interventions with host national security could be at risk. The concerns that SWF investing can be disruptive have gone largely unjustified, and have actually been praised for achieving the opposite in many circumstances. For example, SWFs' heavy investments in crashing financial markets at the time of the global financial crisis (GFC) of 2007–2008 actually helped mitigate their collapse. Now, as the world is paying more attention to diversify its investment portfolio and address critical concerns of sustainability, significant SWF capital has entered new sectors such as those of infrastructure, green energy and renewables, telecommunications, port management, cultural heritage, water management, education, and even entertainment.

The purpose of this study is to explore the various setups and mandates of SWFs, and their investment strategies that possess sustainable footprints on their internal and external ecosystems. With a qualitative methodology depending on (review of documents) content analysis, secondary data collection, and in-depth interviews with SWF executives, this study sheds light on their governance frameworks and the tools by which they are assessed accordingly. The study also aims to explore how could state-owned SWFs harness their financial resources to address sustainable development, without compromising their profit-seeking objectives? To what extent do SWFs particularly from EMs contribute to the free float of investment capital across countries? And finally, what are some of the lessons learned from key EMs and their respective SWFs that could be valuable takeaways?

Given the multiple sources of information the Element resorted to, the study presents its main findings and policy recommendations for concerned stake-holders. Main findings tap on the fact that SWF proliferation in the past decade could be attributed to (in some cases) sudden resource discoveries and spikes in export earnings; counterreactions to worldwide crises (such as the GFC and COVID-19 pandemic to enhance resilience); structural reforms in owner states or directives to address sustainability issues more seriously. Irrespective to the triggers, SWFs have proven to be viable business models for countries with excess resource earnings and have helped achieve sustainable development for present and future generations. The historic suspicion toward SWFs has diminished over the years as they have worked hard to solidify their legitimacy and showcase their prominent participation in global financial markets.

With respect to EMs, they could deploy their diverse mandates to address both domestic and international objectives of economic growth and financial returns. Each EM enjoys a basket of attributes that grants it a particular competitive edge. These attributes could assist it in spurring domestic economic development and at the same time serve as an attractive reason for foreign capital to dive in. Challenges of governance, resilience, and sustainability have been overcome successfully among many EM (SWF) owners, yet ample room for improvement still remains. In most of the cases explored in this research, relatively weak governance standards in SWFs varied and exposed how lack of transparency about management structures and decision-making processes could cost SWFs lots of potential investments it could otherwise embark on. Unfortunately, SWFs that do not commit to sound transparency measures are at risk of cronyism or even accusations of corruption.

1.2 Identifying the Nature of Sovereign Wealth Funds (SWFs)

SWFs can be defined as pools of capital often derived from natural resources or trade earnings. They are government funds that manage national savings, budget surplus, and excess foreign exchange reserves by investing them globally into corporate stocks and bonds and other financial instruments. "These foreign currency assets are managed separately from the official reserves of the monetary authorities. However, whether these foreign assets are part of the reserve assets of a country is hitherto ambiguous. Thus viewed, a SWF is the investment vehicle of a Sovereign government that holds foreign assets for long-term purposes" (Das, 2009).

The International Monetary Fund (IMF) defines SWFs as special purpose investment funds owned by the government for macroeconomic purposes (Yu & Yang, 2017). Academically, the Sovereign Wealth Fund Institution (SWFI) defines SWFs to be state-owned investment funds or entities that are commonly established from balance of payments (BoPs) surpluses, official foreign currency operations, the proceeds of privatization, and/or receipts resulting from commodity export earnings (IMF, 2007; Sovereign Wealth Fund Institute, 2008). Unlike pension funds, SWFs are not financed with contributions from pensioners and do not have a stream of liabilities committed to individual citizens (Elbadawi & Zaki, 2020). SWFs reflect the accumulation of wealth of nations. Those countries establishing SWFs usually experience wealth expansion from economic progress mostly in the form of foreign exchange surplus revenue. The definition of SWF excludes, among other things (1) foreign currency reserve assets held by monetary authorities for the traditional BoPs or monetary policy purposes; (2) state-owned enterprises (SOEs) in the traditional sense; (3) government employee pension funds (funded by employee/employer contributions); or (4) assets managed for the benefit of individuals (Sovereign Wealth Fund Institute, 2008).

Realistically, the bulk of SWFs are centered in oil-rich and exporting countries (e.g., Libya,[1] Saudi Arabia, Kuwait, United Arab Emirates (UAE), and, last but not least, Qatar), and East Asia (like Singapore and Malaysia). It is often easy to categorize SWFs dichotomously into commodity-based funds and non-commodity-based ones. As the name entails, commodity sovereign funds are created from the excess earnings resulting from large export scales for either one or a basket of commodities. In most cases, these export earnings come from oil, gas, and precious metals (as in the case of the Botswana Pula Fund based on the export proceeds of diamonds) and raise the value of AUM[2] in their respective funds. Non-commodity funds, on the other hand, are typically financed from currency reserves or current account surpluses, driven by corporate or household saving rates.

In 2008, a group of twenty-three leading state-owned international investors from around the world established the International Forum of Sovereign Wealth Funds (IFSWF). Often referred to as the Kuwait Declaration, the IFSWF became a voluntary organization of global SWFs committed to working

---

[1] The Libyan Investment Authority (LIA) was established in 2006 according to the IFSWF governance principles. Its mandates include domestic development and future-generation savings. According to its official website, the last valuation of its AUM was done in 2012 and stood at US$67 billion. No further record has been disclosed since. Despite being a full member of the IFSWF, the LIA has been long known for its low records on the Truman Governance Scorecard.

[2] AUM is the total market value of the investments that are managed on behalf of clients.

together and strengthening the community through dialogue, research, and self-assessment. In the same year, the IFSWF's precursor, the International Working Group of Sovereign Wealth Funds, met with global groups, such as the G20, IMF, and the US Department of the Treasury, and drafted a set of generally accepted principles and practices (GAPPs), known as the Santiago Principles, for SWFs' institutional governance and risk-management frameworks. These are a set of twenty-four GAPPs that aim at promoting transparency, good governance, accountability, prudent investment practices, open dialogue, and a deeper understanding of the SWF operations (Tsani & Overland, 2020). Following the Kuwait Declaration in 2009, the International Working Group became the IFSWF with the mandate of helping members implement the Principles (IFSWF, 2021c). Technically, the IFSWF operates in an inclusive manner and facilitates communication among SWFs, as well as with recipient country officials, and representatives of multilateral organizations and the private sector. Through its work, the IFSWF contributes to the development and maintenance of an open and stable investment environment, thereby supporting the four guiding objectives underlying the Santiago Principles.[3]

Sovereign countries create SWFs, and these are special SOEs that often add fiscal instruments to the government toolbox and are proactive tools in sustaining host countries' national objectives. They serve multiple purposes, some of which include insulating the budget and economy from excess volatility in revenues; helping monetary authorities diffuse unwanted liquidity; building up savings for future generations, or using the money for economic and social development. Ideally, SWFs are to operate on market principles and are expected to follow international market rules. This entails being immune to any political stance or orientation imposed on it by its respective government, or any other state entity for that matter. Although having diverse legal, institutional, and governance structures, SWFs manage assets by employing a set of investment strategies and take risks to achieve financial objectives, often by separate organizations than the central banks. All of the previous elements of SWFs echo the current financial market liberalism (Yu & Yang, 2017). Figure 1 below displays some of the largest SWFs in the world, ranked according to their volumes of assets under management (Global SWF, 2022).

---

[3] These are (1) to help maintain a stable global financial system and free flow of capital and investment; (2) to respect and abide by all data disclosure requirements in host countries in which they invest; (3) to invest on the basis of economic and financial risk and return-related considerations only with no political objectives involved; and (4) to practice adequate transparency and governance guidelines to ensure accountability and monitoring of investment operations.

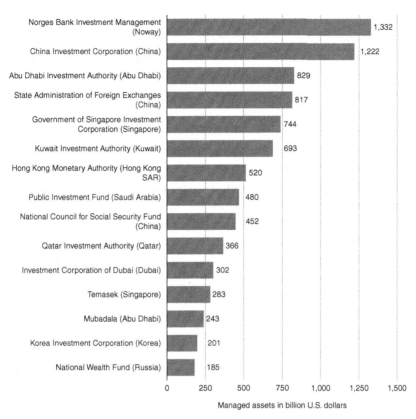

Figure 1 Largest SWFs worldwide as of January 2022, by assets under management (in billion US dollars).
Source: Global SWF (2022).

2 Types of Sovereign Funds

There are a few traditional classifications of SWFs. These include: First, stabilization funds that carry a primary objective to insulate the budget and the economy against transient phenomena such as commodity price swings and the volatility of their prices. Stabilization funds are created to assist in balancing short-term fiscal positions for a government and act as an additional macroeconomic policy tool for meeting government payments and foreign exchange commitments in countries with less-developed capital markets and/ or pegged currencies (Sharma, 2017). SWFs with such mandate are intended to smooth fiscal gaps in domestic budgets and are therefore restrained by underlying liability arrangements that depend on fiscal deficits (Kalter & Shena, 2013).

Second, savings funds (for future generations), which aim to convert nonrenewable assets into a more diversified portfolio of assets. As the name entails, these funds are set up with the objective of investing excess reserves for the benefit of future generations. The source of these savings funds usually goes back to rare swings of commodity prices. They are also used as a supplement to foreign exchange reserves and are run by a country's central bank. The main objective behind savings funds is to allow a window for risky investments that may generate once in a generation boost in returns.

Third, reserve investment corporations, which are established to increase the return on reserves. They aim to reduce the negative carry costs of holding reserves or to earn higher return on ample reserves, while keeping the assets in the funds as-is (e.g., China, South Korea, and Singapore) (Al-Hassan et al., 2013).

Fourth, are development funds which typically help fund socioeconomic projects or promote industrial policies that raise a country's potential output growth. They are directed toward national projects such as infrastructure and often aim to crowd-in foreign institutional investor capital. Development funds have also been termed "strategic investment funds." These exist when typically, 50 percent or more of their investments are in national companies (i.e., defined as a private equity stake) (Hentov & Petrov, 2015). These funds may involve earmarking excess revenues for specific domestic investments like transportation and water infrastructure projects, healthcare development assignments, and education schemes. Such earmarking can be an approach of preventing politically driven spending decisions from bypassing the natural budgeting process. Earmarking involves withdrawing money from a sovereign fund, usually a natural resource one, and requiring that it be spent on specific expenditure items through the budget process (Onifade, 2016). Last but not least, the fifth classification is contingent pension reserve funds, which are derived from sources other than individual pension contributions and provide for contingent unspecified pension liabilities on the government's balance sheet (Meng, 2020).

With this assortment comes a variety of objectives and mandates that SWFs carry. These objectives include multiple macroeconomic and political standpoints such as protecting and stabilizing the budget and the economy from volatility shocks in revenues/exports; diversifying from nonrenewable commodity exports; earning greater returns on foreign exchange reserves; assisting monetary authorities to dissipate unwanted liquidity; funding social and economic development; and last but not least, shaping a country's political strategy.

SWFs receive their funding either from transfers of oil/natural gas revenues earned by national energy companies or from transfers of excess foreign exchange reserves earned from exports and managed by the country's central bank or Treasury. For this reason, SWFs are often referred to as either "oil based" or "trade surplus based." Nevertheless, there are other important methods of categorizing SWFs, which help explain their investing behavior, operating philosophy, and how they are received by nations targeted for SWF investment – whether the funds are sponsored by democratic or nondemocratic nations and, closely related, whether the funds operate in a transparent or nontransparent manner (Bortollotti et al., 2015). The rationale, objectives, and investment behavior of SWFs are identical to other funds like trust, hedge, or private equity funds. However, as the assets of SWFs belong to a Sovereign nation, managed through an ad hoc fund, these funds are aptly christened SWFs. Although little is known about the nature and degree of government intervention in the operations of individual SWFs, the majority of them are largely semiautonomous, self-directed entities, dedicated to professional portfolio management (Griffith-Jones & Ocampo, 2011).

The inception of most SWFs, however, is not – and should not be – linked to political motivations but the primary result of macroeconomic considerations. Wealth funds might seem an excellent opportunity for nations with high variance in public revenues to ensure steady cash flow levels and provide resources for long-term investments. However, there is a challenging balance when excluding political decisions in managing SWFs, particularly in the emerging world.

The largest SWF in the world on record is The Norwegian Government Pension Fund. According to data from the SWFI, the fund was valued at more than US$1.1 trillion as of January 2021. Most of the assets are tied up in stocks, bonds, and real estate. Next in rank is the China Investment Cooperation fund. It manages a similarly large amount of assets of just above US$1 trillion. The other SWFs in the top eight are not nearly as big. The difference between the third place (UAE) and second is substantial. In general, most funds are located in Asia and the Arab world – in Hong Kong, China, Singapore, as well as Saudi Arabia, Kuwait, and the UAE.[4]

The unique Norwegian fund was set up to invest government revenues from fossil-fuel industries into sectors deemed more sustainable in order to provide for a future when the country can no longer rely on its income from oil. The Norwegian government is free to use up to 3 percent of the fund's volume annually for social purposes – that number currently amounts up to US$33 billion.[5]

On the Asian front, China has had a steady growth in its trade surpluses from export earnings. Progressively rising oil and gas prices, on the other hand, have

---

[4] www.statista.com/chart/24060/the-worlds-biggest-sovereign-wealth-funds/, Accessed July 27, 2021

[5] www.statista.com/chart/24060/the-worlds-biggest-sovereign-wealth-funds/, Accessed July 27, 2021.

increased the revenues of the Gulf Cooperation Council (GCC) and the Russian Federation and turned them into globally significant net investors. In this subgroup of economies, China has been the largest global investor, with almost twice as much foreign investment as the next largest emerging market economy (EME) – the Russian Federation – and three times as much as the Republic of Korea (herein after Korea), the third-largest investing EME. Economies that are Asia's financial hubs, namely, Hong Kong SAR, Singapore, and Taiwan, have strengthened their bond with the EMEs of the region, and are expanding global investment rapidly (Das, 2009).

2.1 A Closer Look at Domestic Development, Stabilization, and Savings SWFs

SWFs are meant to bring stability to government finances or provide long-term economic stimulus. They could act as a helping arm to traditional monetary and fiscal policy tools (macroeconomic policies) that administer taxes, government spending, money supply, interest rates, among other tools. Despite the multiple similarities present among SWFs, there are many striking differences when it comes to size, goals, and levels of sophistication. SWFs typically have one of three goals: stability, savings for future generations, or domestic development. These goals often vary based on the SWF's source(s) of capital and the needs of the entity controlling it (Ouni & Plaisent, 2020). Ultimately, in a lot of cases, SWFs have been established to manage natural resource-derived revenues, yet in others, they may not be linked explicitly to the latter and have been established to manage BoP surpluses in countries with no natural resources. Literature broadly points to two important prerequisites for establishing a resource-based SWF, namely, the expectation of large capital inflows and existing low public debt (Mulder et al., 2009). Importantly, if a country suffers high public debts, it is usually advisable to first pay them off to improve borrowing terms and international credit ratings and only then consider establishing a fund.

Nevertheless, the core objective behind their creation resides in protecting and stabilizing the budget and economy, especially at times when export earnings are excessively volatile due to price swings. Afterall SWFs are meant to ensure long-term growth of capital and diversification of the local basket of exports (particularly nonrenewable commodities).

SWFs are not sensitive only to risk-return considerations like other traditional (or market-focused) institutional investors. One major distinctive feature is their long-term investment horizon as they have no short-term liabilities; they maximize their risk-adjusted returns and diversify their portfolios across asset classes, industries, and geographies (Arouri et al., 2018).

The investment and development objectives are expected to have different portfolio allocation implications, and a rich ongoing financial literature tests the validity of the two hypotheses (Grira, 2020). Previous work on the motives behind SWFs deals was subject to empirical investigation and showed that, in some cases, politics do interfere (Murtinu & Scalera, 2016), but in most cases, SWFs transactions are dealt with as rational institutional investors (Liu & Price, 2020). It has also been shown that, compared to other institutional investors, SWFs are more likely to target firms operating in strategic sectors (Boubakri et al., 2016). According to the Organization of Economic Cooperation and Development (OECD), SWFs are welcomed as constructive contributions to recipient countries' economic development (Lorfing, 2021). To date, they have been reliable, long-term, and commercially driven investors and a force for global financial stability. The international organization has also recognized that if SWF investments were motivated by political rather than commercial objectives, they could be a source of concern, and that legitimate national security concerns could arise. The latter also welcomed international discussions involving SWFs, their governments, and recipient governments. These increase understanding, contribute to mutual trust and confidence, and help avoid protectionist responses that could undermine economic growth and development.

Going back to SWFs with stabilization mandates in resource-rich countries, it is worth noting that such lucrative revenues are often subject to price and supply volatility. Given the correlation between commodity prices and their supply, while small price swings may occur frequently, significant fluctuations hit more rarely but with longer periods of spillover effects. The discovery of natural factor endowments, as in the case of Ghana in 2007, can therefore have a de-stabilizing effect on a country's budget cycle, leading to disproportionate and inefficient spending during resource booms and budget shortfalls during busts (Dixon & Monk, 2011).

Ideally, economic theory would argue that stabilization ought to be achieved via sound management of traditional macroeconomic policies[6] rather than resorting to withdrawals from an SWF. In the case of many emerging and developing countries, unimpressive macroeconomic performance indicators have caused withdrawal constraints that are usually heightened during commodity price falls. Other emerging economies with better macroeconomic performances, as

---

[6] Such as fiscal and monetary policies, which could be administered either pro-cyclically or countercyclically. General countercyclical fiscal policy can be carried out through automatic stabilizers, as well as by paying down debt in boom times and borrowing in times of recession (Markowitz, 2020). Meanwhile, pro-cyclical monetary policy instruments can alleviate the externalities of currency exchange fluctuations and demand shocks by adopting expansionary measures at times of economic booms and contractionary ones at times of recessions.

in the case of some Arab Gulf states like the UAE, prefer to resort to conventional budgetary measures to relieve their economy from a recession or provide anti-inflationary measures should it be racing through an expansion.[7]

Generally speaking, monetary policy tends to be less effective in developing countries if there is poor transmission of the latter to interest and exchange rates, stemming from underdeveloped domestic capital markets or export sectors. Hence, if a country is to wisely handle resource windfalls, it needs politically independent central banks with some degree of autonomy; otherwise, establishing a separate stabilization fund would be the alternative solution. On the other hand, fiscal stabilization funds seek to support countercyclical fiscal policies through "ring-fencing" resource revenues subject to fiscal rules. In other words, a straightforward fiscal rule would tie any government withdrawals, and deposits, into an SWF to a resource "reference" price or benchmark. This link would allow for withdrawals should current market prices fall below this benchmark, and conversely, call for deposits if revenues were above the reference price. This way, stabilization funds can stockpile extra earnings at times of revenue hikes and can be used to be drawn upon at times of revenue plunges (Bauer & Mihalyi, 2018).

Unfortunately, there is no golden fiscal rule prescription that can be generalized. Yet, establishing an enforceable one with little room for loopholes is crucial for stabilization funds to operate effectively (Markowitz, 2020). If not, political pressure would find its way into SWF agendas and would highly influence their mandates. Lessons have proven that SWFs with market orientations are more credible, as they are driven by high-risk high-return investments. As stabilization funds tend to rely on the readiness of funds whenever necessary; as the name entails, they require some degree of liquidity. Hence, most if not all stabilization SWFs move toward short-term investment plans, incorporating more dilute financial instruments, as in the case of Treasury bills. These funds function as an alternative to external borrowings at times of economic recessions. Finally, applying solid fiscal rules to stabilization funds renders itself fruitless if such solidity is not mirrored onto the general budget, especially if SWF revenues do not comprise a large percentage of the country's gross domestic product (GDP) (Wills, 2018).

With respect to SWFs that incorporate saving mandates, it is difficult to refute the logic behind them, which emphasizes the importance of extending resource earnings to future generations and not only to current ones. To mitigate the effect of overconsuming resource revenues by current generations, countries

---

[7] The UAE adheres to a pegged exchange rate system that somehow limits its authority over its own monetary policy.

often resort to capital investments. By investing resource revenues in capital, which translates into permanent income and continues to grow even after resources have been depleted, this conundrum could be resolved. Stemming from this logic, savings funds seek to invest resource wealth in long-term assets (often abroad), in order to spread current wealth more evenly over time to benefit future generations (Carney, 2021). Ultimately, savings funds aim to share the wealth of a country across generations by investing in a portfolio of higher risk-return investments. The investment returns on these funds can then be used to finance government expenditure once oil or minerals are depleted. In summary, the retained earnings from commodity sales that are injected into savings funds are eventually converted into more sustainable and "longer-duration" financial assets.

For example, Singapore's Temasek and Malaysia's Khazanah SWFs were both established with funds raised via the sale of government-owned companies (Carney, 2021). The advantage of possessing savings SWFs is that they encounter the smallest number of restrictions on their capacity to engage in strategic investments because they are not specifically targeted for any future-funding obligations. The longer investment horizon of savings funds allows them to benefit from the illiquidity premium[8] (Amihud et al., 2015). In summary, savings funds retain a big appetite for large-scale and long-term ownership stakes in both domestic and foreign firms, thereby yielding the highest potential for active interventions in invested firms among all SWF categories (Amihud et al., 2015).

Table 1 displays an overview of sovereign investors, their sources of funding, mandates, and business models.

3 The Proliferation of SWFs

While SWFs have existed since the middle of the twentieth century, their notoriety has increased substantially over the past twenty years as a result of their intense accumulation of assets. In 2000, SWFs held about US$1 trillion against a total estimated at over US$7 trillion in 2015 (Elbadawi et al., 2018). The influx of SWFs that emerged in the past few decades was due to a commodity boom that took place in many Middle Eastern and African countries, mainly the Gulf region, Norway, and many others. Going back in history, research shows how two economic phenomena have promoted the

---

[8] A liquidity premium is any form of additional compensation that is required to encourage investment in assets that cannot be easily and efficiently converted into cash at fair market value. For example, a long-term bond will carry a higher interest rate than a short-term bond because it is relatively illiquid.

Table 1 An overview of sovereign investors

Type of sovereign investor	Source of funding	Mandate	Business model	SWF – by country
Sovereign Wealth Fund	• Resource revenues • Excess foreign currency reserves	• Macroeconomic stability • Investing sovereign wealth toward domestic development	• Stabilization: investments in highly liquid yet fixed-income portfolios. Stabilization funds tend to adopt asset allocations heavily oriented to cash and fixed-income securities and avoid less-liquid assets with minimum risk • Saving: long-term returns; highly diversified portfolios	• Norwegian Government Pension Fund • Abu Dhabi Investment Authority (ADIA) – UAE • China Investment Corporation • Kuwait Investment Authority
Central banks	• Foreign exchange reserves	• Management of exchange rates to maintain stability of prices and inflation	• Highly liquid (liquid equities) • Fixed-Income returns • Minimum diversification	• National central banks • People's Bank of China • Saudi Arabian Monetary Agency

| Pension fund | • Fiscal previsions and surplus contributions | • Asset pools with long-term liabilities | • Long-term returns
• Maximum diversification
• Illiquid assets | • Australia Future Fund
• Canadian Public Pension Investment Board
• Korean National Pension Fund |
| Development banks | • Government transfers
• Debt-equity financing | • Sectors with growth potential. High returns | • Diversified asset portfolio
• Public and private equity assets
• Infrastructure projects
• Public–private partnerships (PPPs) | • Mubadala – UAE
• The Sovereign Fund of Egypt (TSFE)
• Temasek – Singapore
• Public Investment Fund (PIF) – Saudi Arabia |

Source: Author; based on Alsweilem et al. (2015).

growth of SWFs since 1999. The first was the massive accumulation of foreign (mostly dollar-denominated) official reserves by central banks that were triggered by the shattering 1997–1998 East Asian financial crisis (Young, 2020). According to the World Bank (WB), governments have built up increasingly massive foreign exchange reserve holdings over the years, and this has prompted them to reallocate some assets to SWFs, to seek a commercial return without having to convert out of dollars. The second major force fueling the recent growth of SWFs has been the nearly unstoppable rise in the world price of oil, which increased from barely US$10 per barrel in 1998 to over US$148 a decade later, before stabilizing between US$90 and US$110 per barrel since 2010 (Stocker et al., 2018). Recently, a shift of investment strategies away from traditional reserve currencies (e.g., dollar, yen) to emerging currencies and stocks (public equities, private firms, as well as real estate investments) was evidently recorded.

Reverting to the analysis of why SWFs have risen in both number and volume across African countries and other emerging economies is the rise of democracy. With more democratic institutions accommodating larger numbers of veto players in public policymaking processes, SWFs get to be endorsed and promoted. Democracy actually promotes SWF institutionalization by its need for a strong rule of law, voters defying unfavorable pressures imposed by politicians, and the free flow of information, and vice versa (Wang & Li, 2016). However, the rise of democratic rule is not the only megatrend impacting the proliferation of SWFs. There are multiple megatrends that have influenced both the creation and the objectives of the latter. These trends could possess social, economic, or even political attributes but have succeeded in shaping both current and future outlooks.

Demographic and social changes encountered in many nations, such as aging populations and inversed population pyramids, have impacted the approach nations plan for their future. More emphasis on sustaining near-term resource revenues is clearly seen across aging demographics, with special interest toward maximizing the benefits of current soon-to-be depleted resources. With the recent surge of earnings in resource-rich countries across EMs, it is evident how economic and commercial power has shifted toward the latter. This has led to a surge in the investment appetite of sovereign institutions and has also granted emerging economies a new yet distinct role in shaping worldwide investment trends.

The rising interest and awareness of SWFs' benefits and leverage powers have also been substantially affected by spreading trends of state capitalism. State-led investments are now shedding off their skin and deep diving into modern arenas of investments encompassing digital transformation, technology advancements, and other internet-related channels, with the hope of capitalizing on the profitability of these modern investment avenues. Sovereign investors will closely follow the emerging digital trends to capitalize on convergence and industry sector transformation (PwC, 2020).

Furthermore, rapid urbanization has earned its lion's share in attracting sovereign funds toward fixed asset allocations. This has been greatly witnessed in densely populated emerging economies that have suffered from years of urban neglect and collapsing domestic infrastructure. As a tool to attract foreign investments and venture opportunities, sovereign investors in a number of SWF-owner countries (e.g., Egypt) have attempted injecting the latter's returns into their real estate and infrastructure sectors as a way to modernize their investments habitats.

SWFs are also expected to activate and endorse the socially responsible initiatives taken by states to have more environmental, social, and governance (ESG)-driven and sustainable development goals (SDGs)-driven investment profiles. With greater weight given to the social responsibility expected from both the public and private sectors, there has been a tendency to harness SWFs to achieve more favorable targets under the umbrella of sustainable development.

The GFC of 2008–2010 brought the SWFs' aggressive acquisition sprees to light and ever since the Western audience began to give attention to the state-owned investments as a new fiscal tool that could be of substantive advantage. Back then, SWFs from EMs in particular were regarded as liquidity providers to failing economies that were finding it challenging to manage their fiscal and budgetary deficits. These bailout-like moves gave rise to the notion of "state capitalism" as governments began racing to grab acquisition opportunities whenever they manifested themselves. For the first time, EMs exercised unparalleled government intervention to support economies all over the globe during a worldwide crisis. Rising EMs were for once filling in the shoes of their developed predecessors and were injecting lucrative investments in Western crashing markets (Kotter & Lel, 2011).

These mega trends granted special attention to SWFs and subsequently revealed their influence on foreign markets and the domestic economies they were coming from. Both the unprecedented surge in oil prices, followed by an equally aggressive counter drop in the latter left countries to face a record first-time phenomenon of either reaping lump sums resource revenues or filling shocking budgetary gaps. With the COVID-19 health crisis, SWFs were yet again challenged by the perfect storm (Evenett, 2019).

4 Governance of SWFs

The term "governance" can mean many things depending on the context in which it is used. The governance of SWFs refers to the procedures that determine "who does what" in relation to the policies that shape their objectives and mandates, as well as the oversight and accountability of the funds. The successful implementation of SWFs' policies requires coordination between various arms and institutions of government, including ministries (for finance, natural resources, and economic planning), central banks, independent investment authorities, parliament, and public auditors (Alsweilem et al., 2015). Once the term governance is mentioned, the word transparency immediately appears. According to Cumming et al., (2017) there has been immense concern as to the degree of transparency SWFs exercise in general because its absence tends to obfuscate investment agendas, risk-management techniques, and governance. He then went on to confirm the correlation between transparency and the presence of democratic institutional structures and rule of law. Naturally, the stronger the latter, the greater the likelihood of having sound transparent patterns of SWFs. This goes back to the fact that transparent information disclosure allows for holding key investment decision-makers accountable whenever necessary.

There is no doubt that a challenging task exists when excluding political decisions in managing SWFs. Investment mandates based exclusively on commercial frameworks tend to have higher financial returns than if they were politically driven. Highly transparent operations and management of SWFs help in making sound decisions and forward-looking orientations of these funds. Due to the acknowledged importance of transparency, it was therefore highly incorporated in the Santiago Principles. And when countries adopt such Principles, they tend to attract investors.

4.1 Governance Assessment Tools of SWFs: Truman's SWF Governance Scoreboard

According to Clark et al. (2013), the international legitimacy of SWFs is based on the degree to which their design and governance match "Western" expectations about investment management. Clark et al. believed that even small countries with large and globally oriented SWFs are likely to play a significant role in international relations. Therefore, it was considered crucial to closely examine the governance frameworks these SWFs adhered to. Accordingly, the aim of this section is to shed light on the various governance tools adopted by SWFs and the implications these have on investment decisions.

In 2007, Ted Truman from the Peterson Institute for international economics introduced the "Truman Scoreboard" assessing the governance and accountability of SWFs across a number of pillars. Truman granted governance assessment tools great importance that was justified by the unique characteristics SWFs possessed; particularly the undeniable tendency to follow political affiliations adopted by their respective government. As SWFs influenced saving and investment decisions, they were considered tools of wealth accumulation, transferred year-to-year and from generation to generation. With the substantive financial yields they brought home and their rapid proliferation, they have been subject to the world's glare. The growing dominance of SWFs surged many questions related to governance practices that Truman tried to address through his model.

Truman's "Scoreboard" explores five main domains: (1) The possible mismanagement of investments and corruption; (2) The SWF's pursuit of noneconomic or economic-power objectives; (3) Practice of financial protectionism; (4) Financial market instability; and (5) Conflicts of interest.

Once sufficient information about the five domains is provided, it can clearly determine the extent to which governance is exercised. In constructing his index, Truman (2011) groups together the domains into four categories: "(1) structure of the fund, including its objectives, links to the government's fiscal policy, and whether the fund is independent from the countries' international reserves; (2) governance of the fund, including the roles of the government, the board of the fund and its managers, and whether the fund follows guidelines for corporate responsibility; (3) accountability and transparency of the fund in its investment strategy, investment activities, reporting, and audits; and (4) behavior of the fund in managing its portfolio and its risk-management policies, including the use of leverage and derivatives."[9] Each of these makes up an "element" of the Scoreboard, and under each element resides a number of indicators, all carrying a numerical weight that is summed up to reflect a final score out of 100 percentage points. The indicators within each of the four elements are assessed by answering closed ended yes-and-no questions pertaining to the SWF's structure, governance, accountability and transparency, and behavior. The higher the final score, the higher the rank granted to the SWF with respect to its overall governance strategy, and vice versa.[10] Since the

---

[9] Every pillar has a different number of elements or subcategories. For example, the structure subcategory contains eight elements that describe the legal basis of the fund and how it is funded and used. The governance subcategory contains seven elements that describe how the fund operates. The transparency and accountability subcategory groups fourteen elements covering the fund's presentation of information to the public. The behavior category contains four operational elements.

[10] The Scoreboard was edited two years after its initial release in 2009 and currently includes thirty-three elements. By applying the Truman Scoreboard, most SWFs have been put to the

introduction of the scoreboard in 2007 till present, average scores calculated for IFSWF's members have definitely improved. During the same period of time, many have surfaced and have added to the global reservoir of assets under management. It is worth noting that the latter did not increase at the same pace as that of the scores, partly because of frequent withdrawals that financed the spillovers of the COVID-19 crisis. These withdrawals actually imposed more pressure on the real roles SWFs were meant to play. Up to the latest scores released (in 2019),[11,12] data used were derived from the publically disclosed records of assessed SWFs. A challenging fact was the irregular publication of their annual reports, which often came out six months after the beginning of the following year. Other sources of data included official SWFs' websites, their respective ministries of finance, and sometimes international reports such as those published by IMF.

Truman's Scoreboard was somehow similar yet not entirely identical to the Santiago Principles, which were drafted by twenty-three founding states of the IFSWF. Across the thirty-three elements of the Scoreboard, a slack resemblance could be detected within the twenty-four Principles, and vice versa. For example, eight of the thirty-three elements have no trace in the Principles while eight of the Principles have no counterparts in the Scoreboard.[13] A distinct observation could be seen when comparing scoreboard scores to Principles' ratings for the same SWF. A difference in favor of the Santiago Principles grade is usually detected for any given SWF, particularly those belonging to founding states. This could imply more reliability, and accuracy could be found in Truman's Scoreboard, yet the fact that not all elements as well as Principles exist across the two assessment instruments may refute such implication. Table 2 displays Truman's Scoreboard with its main elements based on Stone & Truman (2016).

---

test, all receiving ranks between High, Moderate, and Low rating from 0 to 100 across all thirty-three elements. These thirty-three elements are equally weighted and translated into a percent of 0 to 100. Each element is scored on a 0–1 scale, with partial scores in quarters for some elements.

[11] Truman's Scoreboard was calculated in 2007, 2009, 2012, 2015, and most recently in 2019. The average of scores improved along the years, especially among IFSWF members. Their membership came with obligations to commit to both the Santiago Principles and to improving the records of their governance indicators, particularly with respect to transparency and information disclosure.

[12] On the 2019 SWF scoreboard, the 36 members and associate members of the IFSWF have a slightly higher average (69) than the 28 nonmembers (62). The average for the 16 IFSWF founding members that are still members is higher (76) than the average for all current members; the average for the 7 founding members that dropped out is even higher (80).

[13] The remaining sixteen Principles or their subcomponents roughly match up with twenty-five elements of the SWF scoreboard.

Table 2 Truman's governance scoreboard

Pillar	Elements	Sample of top scoring SWFs by country as of 2019	Name of fund	Total score across all elements
Structure	1. Objective stated	Norway	Norway Government Pension Fund –Global	100
	2. Legal framework	New Zealand	New Zealand Superannuation Funda	94
	3. Changing the structure	USA	Permanent Wyoming Mineral Trust Fund	93
	4. Investment strategy	Chile	Economic and Social Stabilization Fund	92
	5. Source of funding	Azerbaijan	State Oil Fund of the Republic of Azerbaijan	92
	6. Use of fund earnings	Canada	Alberta Heritage Savings Trust Fund	91
	7. Integrated with policies	Timore-Lestea	Petroleum Fund of Timor-Lestea	91
Governance	8. Separate from international reserves	Chile	Pension Reserve Fund	89
	9. Role of government	USA	Alaska Permanent Fund Corporation	88
	10. Role of governing body	Australia	Future Fund	87
	11. Role of managers	USA	New Mexico State Investment Council	87

(Ranks)

Table 2 (cont.)

Pillar	Elements	Sample of top scoring SWFs by country as of 2019	Name of fund	Total score across all elements
	12. Decisions made by managers	Ireland	Ireland Strategic Investment Funda	85
	13. Internal ethical standards	Korea	Korea Investment Corporation	85
	14. Guidelines for corporate responsibility	Palestine	Palestine Investment Fund	85
	15. Ethical investment guideline	Nigeria	Nigeria Sovereign Investment Authority	83
	16. Categories	USA	Alabama Trust Fund	82
	17. Benchmarks	Panama	Fondo de Ahorro de Panamaa	82

Category	# Item	Fund	Country	Score
Transparency and Accountability	18. Credit ratings	Heritage and Stabilization Funda	Trinidad and Tobago	81
	19. Mandates	Temasek Holdings	Singapore	79
	20. Size	Fundo Soberano de Angola	Angola	77
	21. Returns	NSW Generations Fund	Australia	77
	22. Locations	COFIDES	Spain	77
	23. Specific investment	(Texas) Permanent University Fund	USA	77
	24. Currency composition	Mubadala Investment Company	UAE*	75
	25. Annual reports	China Investment Corporation	China	74
	26. Quarterly reports	BPIFrance Investissement	France	74
	27. Regular audits	Caisse des Dépôts et Consignations	France	74
	28. Published audits	CDP Equity/Fondo Strategico Italiano	Italy	70
	29. Independent audits	Dubai Holding	UAE	67
	30. Risk management	ADIA	UAE	65
Behavior	31. Policy on leverage	Investment Corporation of Dubai	UAE	64
	32. Policy on derivatives	National Investment and Infrastructure Funds	India*	62
	33. Portfolio adjustments	Ghana Petroleum Funds	Ghana*	47

*Countries explored in this study as Emerging Economies.
Source: Author's compilation based on Maire et al. (2021a) and Stone et al. (2016).

4.2 The Santiago Principles

In 2008, a group of twenty-three leading state-owned international investors from around the world established the IFSWF.[14] These twenty-three founding members helped draft the Santiago Principles.

Often referred to as the Kuwait Declaration, the IFSWF became a voluntary organization of global SWFs committed to working together and strengthening their community through dialogue, research, and self-assessment. In the same year, the IFSWF's precursor, the International Working Group of Sovereign Wealth Funds, met with global groups such as the G20, IMF, and the US Department of the Treasury and drafted a set of generally accepted principles and practices (GAPPs), known as the Santiago Principles. These Principles dealt with matters pertaining to the SWFs' institutional governance and risk-management frameworks. These are a set of twenty-four GAPPs that aim at promoting transparency, good governance, accountability, prudent investment practices, open dialogue, and a deeper understanding of the SWF operations (Tsani & Overland, 2020). The twenty-four Principles include a total of thirty subprinciples. As of 2020, seven of the twenty-three original IFSWF members are no longer members, including six funds based on natural resources. Following the Kuwait Declaration in 2009, the International Working Group became the IFSWF with the mandate of helping members implement the Principles (IFSWF, 2021c). Today, the forum has thirty-five members and five associate members (Egypt one of them), ten are funds that derive their financing from natural resources (Maire et al., 2021a).

The twenty-four GAPPS revolve around three main core pillars. The first encompasses any given SWFs' legal framework, objectives, and coordination with the macroeconomic policies of the country it is coming from, and that by which it is hosted. This pillar includes ideologies that address the legal structure defining the relationship between the Fund and its government as well as the Fund and its hosting state. These ideologies aim to ensure that objectives of the SWF ultimately support competitiveness in the environment in which they operate whether domestically or internationally; call for greater corporate governance practices; encourage innovation; endorse income diversification for SWF owners; bear pure commercial grounds rather than political ones; and participate in the development of strategic investment schemes that will incorporate sustainability measures and contribute to the achievement of the SDGs.

The second main pillar addresses the institutional framework and governance structure according to which the SWF will adhere. The success of this pillar is contingent to the explicit clarification of the diverse roles and responsibilities of all stakeholders involved in any given investment venture. This is to ensure the facilitation of accountability among involved parties and the emphasis on competencies both required and expected from the latter. Ultimately, the governing body must act in the best interest of the SWF, adhering to all possible ethical and professional standards while doing so. An example of how to execute the ideologies of this principle is making sure that SWFs comply with host countries' regulatory requirements; disclosure mandates included.

The third main pillar of the GAPPs handles investment and risk-management concerns. The Principles derived from this pillar strive to align the investment policies of any given SWF with its disclosed objectives – be it stabilization, savings, domestic development, reserve investment, or even combating symptoms of the Dutch disease.

Sovereign countries manage their SWFs for specific national interests. SWFs add fiscal instruments to the government toolbox and are proactive tools in sustaining host countries' national objectives.

The GFC of 2008 created drastic market changes where institutional investors had to respond by seeking new game-changing modes of investment. SWFs have been no exception. As a matter of fact, the crisis triggered Western governments to welcome SWF investments with open arms, seeing them as rescuers of their collapsing financial markets. However, analysts at the time expressed their concerns that these state-owned SWFs could very much be used to manipulate the political arena of the countries that owned them, hence raising chronic questions about their politicization and governance (Maire et al., 2021a).

According to Liu and Dixon (2019), markets have come to increasingly concede the institutional capacities of SWFs yet they still experience substantial impediments due to the fact that they are government-affiliated investors. Being so, they have had to continuously assert their legitimacy as institutional investors, something their private counterparts rarely, if ever, go through. The ratification of the Santiago Principles along with the IFSWF has been key to proclaim such legitimacy. Both the GAPPs and the Forum endorse all sorts of governance elements such as transparency, accountability, and alignment with macroeconomic policies.

The post-GFC era witnessed a phase where maximization of returns was on top of all market sectors' agenda. Both growth in private equity firms and SWF investment strategies faced amplified regulatory frameworks from host countries. This also coincided with rising SWF domestic development schemes that more often than not overlapped with nationwide industrial policymaking. To make matters more sensitive, sovereign–private partnerships have become increasingly commonplace, raising questions on the validity of the GAPPs and the IFSWF targets. This inevitably led to numerous calls for enhanced transparency and attention to global accountability and scrutiny of the global political economics of SWFs. The GAPPs and IFSWFs were not future-proof.

The primary objective of the Santiago Principles is to reinforce best management and governance practices of free flow of investment capital across borders. They are meant to achieve that without compromising national security concerns emanating from foreign government-affiliated investments. Nevertheless, with the global market transformations that took place, particularly after 2010 and the GFC, propositions of reform were put on the table. Dixon (2019) drafted a conceptual framework that recommended five main reform strategies that would revamp the reliability of the GAPPs, giving them more contemporary-fitted roles in a worldwide dynamic arena. Dixon's conceptual framework advocated the reform based on five main forms of transparency that encompassed: (1) political perspectives, (2) procedural instruments, (3) policy mandates, (4) operational metrics, and (5) performance indicators. These transparency forms tackled the following concerns:

- Rethinking the rigidity of the regulations imposed by host countries on SWF investments, presenting a conflicting stance relative to their announced intentions of domestic growth and development. Regulations in host countries need to be more cohesive and accommodating to both local legitimacy and SWF investment inflows. Unfortunately, the rise of greater strictness on foreign investment in some host countries highlights the lack of policy mapping between host-country regulators and SWFs. This is a paradoxical development, given the original policy agenda that gave way to the Santiago Principles in the first place. The rise of such phenomenon is due to the national security concerns that host countries express because of the possible intervention emanating from foreign investments. These concerns actually catalyzed the rigidity of host countries' investment policies that conflicted with the original mandate of the Principles altogether. Such conflicting objectives will call for reforms that will need to have a dual trajectory of honoring the host-country regulations to mitigate against undesirable foreign investment, while expediting the Principles' promotion of free flow of investment capital. In order to achieve this balance, calls for greater transparency are simply indispensable to avoid the dilemmatic operation between host countries and SWFs.
- Policy relevance of the GAPPs to the dynamics of contemporary market trends needs to be revised, allowing for more agility and resilience to sustain SWFs investments and make them embrace the evolving investment environment.
- Acknowledging the potential partnership models proposed by SWFs institutions and pushing forward for the possible mutual benefits to be reaped from such collaborations. This would reinforce the regular assessment of the performance of the investments made and shed light on the investment outcomes

achieved from the fund. Such performance-related transparency would entail the disclosure of performance metrics and indicators that would facilitate both the measurement and evaluation of actual results, while comparing them to a market benchmark whenever possible. It would also include announcing the processes by which external auditing is executed and how qualitative assessments of the Fund's investment outcomes are made.

- Activating sovereign–private partnerships over and above sovereign–sovereign. The Santiago Principles would legitimate such arrangements, giving ample room for improved transparency and disclosure of information. This operational transparency would require the disclosure of all manners by which assets under the funds' management are administered and accumulated.
- Routinizing the periodic revision and reassessment of the reliability of the Santiago Principles with the aim of continuously ensuring they are in synchronization with modern market needs. Such periodic revision should not be seen as revolutionary, but rather an execution of the twenty-fourth principle itself. GAPP 24 actually supports the regular review of the implementation of the Principles.

Based on Dixon's 2013 review on enhancing the transparency dialogue of the GAPPs (2013), compliance with the Principles has been slow and incomplete. This emphasizes the natural political nature of SWFs, as they reflect the norms and conventions of their government sponsors in regard to transparency. However, compliance is a two-way road that relies on the goodwill of both the state-owned SWF and the host environment in which it flows into. When there are discrepancies in the required standards of such compliance, matters get sensitive and complicated between all parties. Hence, it is crucial to expedite an explicit agreement on disclosure and transparency terms among all stakeholders, and better still, provide clear justification as to when nondisclosure is permitted. If any party ruminates the legitimacy of nondisclosure on certain investment agendas (SWFs' withdrawals and injections included for that matter), it is only fair to assert that such nondisclosure should not by any means be a way to demean the importance of the contrary in other domains, let alone abide by such legitimacy claims. The ultimate target in such a scenario is to encourage dialogue, in concurrence with the Santiago Principles, on nondisclosure as doing so leads to increased transparency overall. Said slightly differently, "dialogue on nondisclosure is, in itself, a form of transparency" (Dixon, 2013).

4.3 The L–M Index

Since the release of the Santiago Principles and the first SWF scoreboard, researchers have created other rating systems, including the Linaburg Maduell

Transparency Index (LMTI). The Index was actually developed by the Institute of Sovereign Wealth Funds by Carl Linaburg and Michael Maduell in 2008. Since then, it has been used by SWFs around the world and included in their disclosed public reports as a standard benchmark of transparency and "ethical" outlook. The Index encompasses ten main criteria that reflect an SWF's transparency to its public, as shown in Table 3. Each criterion is graded on a scale of 1–10, 1 being the lowest possible rank an SWF could score. The methodology by which the grade is given is left to the complete discretion of the Institute of Sovereign Wealth Funds. However, the Institute recommends a minimum score of 8 in order to confidently claim transparency standards are sufficiently met.

Some striking similarities across all instruments remain irreplaceable such as aspects related to the disclosure of background information (including mandates, origins of wealth, and government ownership structure), which are focal points in the L–M Index, for example. Also, the provision of periodically audited reports (covering details such as ownership percentage of company holdings, geographic locations of holdings, total portfolio market value, returns, and management compensation) remains intact among all scales, particularly the L–M Index. Finally, each of the SWF Scoreboard developed by Truman, the IFSWF Santiago Principles, and the L–M Index grant high importance to the

Table 3 The Linaburg–Maduell transparency index

+Point	Principles of Linaburg–Maduell Transparency Index
+Point	1. Fund provides history including reason for creation, origins of wealth, and government ownership structure
+Point	2. Fund provides updated independently audited annual reports
+Point	3. Fund provides ownership percentage of company holdings and geographic locations of holdings
+Point	4. Fund provides total portfolio market value, returns, and management compensations
+Point	5. Fund provides guidelines in reference to ethical standards, investment policies, and enforcers of guidelines
+Point	6. Fund provides clear strategies and objectives
+Point	7. Fund clearly identifies subsidiaries and contact information
+Point	8. Fund identifies external managers
+Point	9. Fund manages its own website
+Point	10. Fund provides main office location address and contact information

Source: Author, based on the Linaburg–Maduell Transparency Index (LMTI); IFSWF, 2021b.

degree by which SWF investment adhere to ethical and sustainable standards when it comes to drafting their investment policies.

In principle, the LMTI identifies high-achieving funds (such as that of Norway and New Zealand) based on their transparency measures, structure, and responsible investment strategies.

Nevertheless, these quantitative approaches to measure the degree of governance do not come without faults. Generalizing the application of the indexes, with the L–M or Truman Scoreboard, tends to possess a subjective nature to their rubrics and a tendency to be biased in favor of economies of a more advanced nature. For demonstration, each principle assessed within the L–M Index incorporates different levels of "depth" and hence judgments that are expressed at the SWF Institute's own freedom. The absence of impartial qualitative assessments makes such bias multifolded due to the fact that SWFs are themselves required to evaluate their own constituents. The fact that the data needed to compile such indexes and scoreboards come from the SWFs themselves raises red flags of conflicting interest and even more bias that are subsequently mirrored on the achieved results and rankings. Hence, there is ample room for improvement in terms of objectiveness of assessment methodologies. With respect to the L–M Index in particular, Table 3 depicts how it focuses on data disclosure, and how it calls for the practice of both internal and external reporting. The distinction between the two pertains to the audience to which reports are targeted. While internal reporting composes an integral part of the governance structure of an SWF itself, external reporting is that done to stakeholders outside the SWF's governance structure, including the general public. In doing so, an SWF renders itself transparent and alleviates its legitimacy to the external universe. The more accurate and timely external reporting is conducted, the more an SWF answers concerns of economic and financial orientation, financial markets' stability, and, last but not least, trust among countries hosting their investments. This in turn feeds into the degree by which an SWF complies with both international and domestic regulations, and again, improves perceptions toward its legitimacy. In doing so, Index scores get to be placed under the intense scrutiny of external entities, and will subsequently impact the objectivity by which the grades are given in the first place. Furthermore, external reporting can be improved by embedding future-driven analyses of investment strategies. This means providing comprehensive outlooks of the SWF's investment mandates, asset allocation, and expected returns on investment.[15] Ultimately, to satisfy a broader base of external stakeholders, it

---

[15] Of course, the more these are oriented toward sustainable projects with ethical outcomes to both citizens and environment, the more they will contribute to the Fund's status and legitimacy.

is highly recommended to also report expected returns across extended periods of time, for example, up to twenty years. Such projections could possess a more realistic characteristic to them and will contribute to more long-term stability in international financial markets. In the end, with the application of sound governance structures and external reporting, Transparency indexes in general, not only the L–M Index, will render themselves more objective and reliable.

4.4 The GSR Scoreboard

In July 2020, the Global SWF introduced a new index that not only provided a more comprehensive coverage of the governance quality and sustainability efforts of SWFs and PPFs but also introduced the concept of resilience to the assessment. As depicted in Table 4 (Megginson et al., 2020), this Governance–Sustainability–Resilience (GSR) Scoreboard comprises twenty-five different

Table 4 The GSR governance scorecard

Governance – ten elements	Sustainability – ten elements	Resilience – five elements
Mission and vision	Ethical standards and policies	Risk management policy
Deposit and withdrawal rules	Stewardship team in place	Strategic asset allocation
External manager reputation	Economic mission	Policy for withdrawals
Internal and external governance	Economic impact and measure	business continuity management (BCM/ Crisis) teams in place
Investment strategy/ criteria	ESG annual report	Speed and discipline
Structure and operational data	Alignment with SDGs	
Annual accounts audited	Partnership and memberships	
AUM figure public	Emerging Markets/ managers	
details of investment portfolio	Role in domestic economy	
Annual versus long-term return	ESG risk management	

Source: Based on Megginson et al. (2020).

elements or rather questions, ten of them related to Governance issues, ten to Sustainability concerns, and five related to Resilience matters.[16] The questions are closed ended yes/no ones, similar to those of Truman's SWF Scoreboard, and have equal weight where the results are converted to a percentage for any given Fund being assessed (Wurster & Schlosser, 2021). According to the IFSWF (2021b) score, the GSR Scoreboard is applied to 100 major state-owned investors (SOIs) annually, generating 2,500 data points. Its rating system functions as a critical tool of analysis that helps in identifying best practices and also points out areas of improvement. Being as transparent as it is, it serves all stakeholders involved with a scrutinized picture of the intricate details of an investment state-owned fund.

Since its introduction, the GSR Scoreboard aims to act as a new market reference for the governance, sustainability, and resilience efforts undertaken (or failed to) by certain state-owned funds.

The global events that took place in global markets could act as an explanation for the Scoreboard's emergence and rationale. Since the GFC in 2008, SWFs found a getaway into collapsing foreign markets in the more-developed hemisphere of the world, where mostly EMs had the privilege to finance. At the time, questions pertaining to the objectives of these Funds – where were they to land; which industries will they contribute to; and what sort of investment policies will be tailored for them – were all eye-openers for the dire need to access disclosure to their governance frameworks.

Seven years later, in 2015, more than 190 countries ratified an unprecedented unanimous agreement in Paris to address critical climate change challenges and drafted the seventeen SDGs, and hence funding was badly required. Known as the Paris Agreement, the international organizations chaperoning these SDGs (mainly the United Nations and multiple specialized agencies under its umbrella) turned their attention to the potential funding manifested in the huge reservoirs owned by SWFs of member states. Eventually, sustainability became an increasingly important topic for investors, exerting mounting pressure for them to be not only more transparent but also responsible.[17]

This gave rise to even greater importance to governance and accountability assessment tools, indexes, and metrics, all of which were geared to evaluate how SWFs were performing in those capacities.

---

[16] The first version of GSR Scoreboard was jointly developed by William L. Megginson (University of Oklahoma, University of International Business & Economics (Beijing), Diego Lopez (Global SWF LLC), and Asif Malik (University of Oklahoma) in 2020.

[17] Some of these investors are now signatory members of the Principles for Responsible Investing (PRI), of the One Planet SWF Group, and/or of the Net Zero Asset Owner Alliance, among others. The PRI produces annual qualitative assessments of state-owned investments.

In 2020, the world was struck by yet another shocking event; the COVID-19 pandemic that tested the resilience and survival abilities of countries around the globe. With mass-scale lockdowns and entire sectors closing doors, huge disappointing setbacks of what was already challengingly achieved of the SDG targets were inevitable. This exacerbated stubborn funding gaps and imposed even more pressure on institutional investors. With such setbacks, countries' and investors' resilience was aggressively tested. Becoming of exceptional importance among the Global SWF community, assessing resilience was helpful in shedding light on the latter's sophistication and internal capabilities (Liang & Renneboog, 2020). These events brought institutional investors to crossroads where transparency and accountability, sustainability and resilience were all being questioned; and the winners were those who balance out the equation across all three capacities, with minimum compromise; and here came the role of the GSR Scoreboard.[18] With a track record of two years only this far, the GSR Scoreboard points out an interesting observation that of which public pension funds (PPFs)[19] (although not of primary focus in this element) score on average much higher than SWFs in any given category. Among them, savings funds tend to be better governed but less responsible, while strategic funds put more effort on the sustainability side.

5 Asset Accumulation and Investment Strategies of SWFs

One of the most important determinants of the long-term growth of SWFs is its savings rule or accumulation process. This accumulation process is meant to build up a principal for a sovereign investment vehicle in anticipation of using its assets and income for a variety of economic purposes (Alsweilem et al., 2015).

To assess the degree of SWFs' contributions to the attainment of development objectives, it is crucial to shed light on the accumulation process of AUM and investment strategies that the latter commonly adopt as a start. It is important to identify the diverse means through which a portion of resource revenues are accumulated and transferred to a separate fund, portfolio, or institution, rather than used for current government spending or held in low-yielding, liquid assets for other short-term macroeconomic policy objectives.

SWFs can be a fundamental component of public asset and liability management and hence play a pivotal role in either maximizing state wealth or abolishing it. With respect to AUM and their accumulation rubrics, there are four main

---

[18] Australia's Future Fund landed the highest scores since the inception of the GSR scoreboard, ranking 1st with a 100 percent total average. Despite keeping a low profile when compared to some of its peers, the Australian federal investor is best in class when it comes to GSR issues.

[19] By nature, pension funds are usually more transparent and accountable than SWFs, given the presence of liabilities and stakeholders.

guidelines that dominate the scene, particularly with respect to funds that depend on resource and commodity revenues. These include (1) fixed percentage transfers, (2) deviations from moving averages, (3) financing of sustainable non-resource fiscal deficits, and (4) reference-price-based accumulation rules.

- Fixed percentage transfers rule: This involves a simple yet rigid rule of transferring a fixed percentage – for example, 10 percent or 20 percent – of annual resource revenues to an SWF. Unless there is a safety clause that freezes the rule during resource revenues falls, these transfers do not depend on commodity prices, revenue cycles, production levels, or the economy. Although this mechanism supports the notion of pro-cyclicality, they have the advantage of being very easy to communicate and difficult to manipulate.
- Deviations from moving averages: A less rigid, more dynamic rule that calls for transferring more revenues to the SWF when prices and revenues exceed the average level of recent years and vice versa. This can result in a volatile, irregular pattern of asset accumulations that will impact investment decisions. Investment options may be restricted to highly liquid outlets with low returns relative to their counterparts.
- Financing of sustainable non-resource fiscal deficits: This rule advocates the automatic transfer of resource revenues to the SWF, which will subsequently reflect onto the budget of an annual amount equivalent to the non-resource fiscal deficit. This rule guarantees that government spending does not depend on inflows of resource revenues from the fund.
- Reference-price-based accumulation rule: Also a less rigid, more counter-cyclical rule that encourages governments and policymakers to select a benchmark price, known as the reference price, to which revenues are linked. Should the world-market price of this commodity rises above the selected reference, the government commits to transferring all resulting revenues to the SWF.[20]

In most SWFs-owner countries, the fund is an integral part of its fiscal framework that encompasses all fiscal policy guidelines. There are a number of complications pertaining to asset–liability management that are derived from (a) volatility and uncertainty of resource revenues, (b) exhaustibility of resource revenues, and (c) Dutch disease symptoms; and these shape the approaches by which governments draw from or inject into their SWFs reservoirs. Nevertheless, injections and withdrawals into and from SWFs should not be confused with numerical fiscal rules. Literature often refers to both terms

---

[20] Such a rule gives the government and policymakers plenty of leeway to regularly adjust the accumulation rule by adjusting the reference price and to pick a conservative, high-accumulation rule (low-reference price) or low-accumulation rule (high-reference price).

interchangeably, assuming that resource-based SWFs are operated under similar, if not identical, fiscal policy rules. Truth is, both are distinct principles with separate guidelines. Numerical fiscal policy rules are those that aim to target one or more indicators in the annual budget, for example, total government spending, debt, or budget balance. By contrast, SWFs injections and withdrawal instructions are based on the framework under which the fund itself is governed (Beuermann et al., 2021). According to the IFSWF, the problem of the policymaker in a resource-rich country can be framed as essentially one of stabilizing domestic fiscal revenue and spending, and ensuring that both can be maintained once the resource is depleted.

6 SWFs and Emerging Economies/Markets (EMs)

The phrase EMs was created by economists in the early 1980s to define investing in developing countries. Most experts agree that the term "emerging market investments" refers to countries or regions undergoing rapid economic growth.

According to the IMF, the circumstances defining EMs are diverse and defy any uniform representation. Although there is no formal definition, EMs are generally classified according to per capita income, exports of diversified goods and services, and greater integration into the global financial system (Duttagupta & Pazarbasioglu, 2021). As an economy becomes richer, it develops, increasing its interaction with the rest of the world while doing so. Yet, this journey is a complex one as it tackles multiple dimensions that will either categorize it as an emerging versus a fully developed nation (Mody, 2003). According to JP Morgan as well as the IMF, there is a set of characteristics that identify EMs. These include macroeconomic indicators (such as the overall size of a nation's economy expressed in nominal GDP, population attributes and demographic profile, and volume of exports relative to the rest of the world), market accessibility (share of global external debt, inclusion in Global Indices, frequency and amount of international bonds issued), and income level (expressed in GDP per capita expressed in nominal dollars).

The WB Group, on the other hand, classifies EMs as either low-income or low-middle-income countries, based on Gross National Income per capita calculated using the Atlas Method. From a more functional approach, EMs are those that have inhibited economic growth due to the institutional voids inflicting their economies. Whether inadequate or not-fully developed public/private institutions, the prevailing cavities contribute to the sluggish macroeconomic advancements EMs face.

Another characteristic of EMs is that they are somehow always in transition, particularly with respect to their demographic profiles. Demographically, EMs are usually transitioning into fluctuating fertility rates, life expectancy patterns, educational attainment spectra, and varying income levels among other factors. Yet, the most important form of transition predominantly witnessed among EMs is the move toward greater interaction with the outside world. Economic activity with the international capital and commodity markets is a trending phenomenon found among numerous EMs. Ultimately, the prevalent transitional phases, volatile markets, and underdeveloped institutional setups in EMs create a rather challenging environment for sound policymaking, particularly in regard to investment mandates.

Over the last two decades, development partners such as the IMF and WB have increasingly encouraged governments in developing countries to establish state-owned investment vehicles (or SWFs) to manage rising resource revenues. The growth of SWFs has been substantial in the last two decades, particularly those with savings objectives, as they have witnessed the fastest-growing category of SWF and currently account for about half of all SWFs. EMs around the world and African countries have recently gained momentum in the field due to recent discoveries of natural resources, mainly oil and gas (as in the case of Ghana in 2007). Despite being geographically distributed in a rather broad manner, yet today, sovereign investment vehicles are heavily concentrated on asset-basis in East Asia and the Middle East regions. With such unprecedented growth patterns of SWFs, the public policy community is now assessing the impact of these investments mainly to help investments flow smoothly across borders, to narrow the gap between resource-rich countries and their counterparts, and, last but not least, to incorporate SWFs objectives as sound fiscal tools in the macroeconomic arena of any given nation.

Ironically enough, with the rising discoveries of fossil-fuel resources in a number of EMs, there is pressing emphasis on the need to reduce the consumption of these environment-unfriendly energy sources. According to the World Economic Forum (2018) and the Climate Change Conference, COP26 held in November 2021,[21] as the rise of renewables and changing patterns of energy use shift the global energy landscape, particularly across the more developed part of the globe, the risk for economies dependent on fossil-fuels revenues continues to climb (World Economic Forum, 2018). Without a shrewd plan to override the overdependence on fossil-fuel energy sources, these nations could be left tied down with an abundance of natural resources, human capacities, infrastructure, and institutions unsuitable for a global road map that incorporates renewable energy to achieve global growth and sustainable development.

---

[21] The 2021 United Nations Climate Change Conference, more commonly referred to as COP26, was the 26th United Nations Climate Change conference, held in Glasgow, Scotland, United Kingdom. The president of the conference was then UK cabinet minister Alok Sharma.

Empirical research has shown that most resource (oil)-rich emerging economies tend to lack the agility and elasticity to respond to future changes due to multiple impediments. The dire need for action to be taken as soon as possible across these countries cannot be more emphasized. However, changes in investment policies will need to be activated and catalyzed by inviting citizens, policymakers, and private-sector investors on board. All segments of society, whether state or non-state actors, are expected to be part of this energy revolution road map.

In line with this thought, there is already a well-established record of government initiatives to deploy private-sector investments and their business models to achieve both financial and sustainable (often including nonfinancial) returns. Terminologies such as public–private partnerships (PPPs), blended finance, or impact investing all advocate for the mobilization of additional finance toward sustainable development, particularly in emerging and developing economies. Among other objectives, these techniques endorse the attraction of commercial capital toward projects that add to the achievement of SDGs while still providing financial rewards to investors. Unfortunately, some studies argue that these terminologies are still in their infancy stages and therefore lack the necessary scale, human capabilities, and market integration strategies needed to mitigate the hazardous impact of fossil-fuel industries.

As emerging economies are uniquely characterized by their rather volatile environments, their volatility is mainly due to their vulnerability when exposed to natural disasters, external price shocks, and general price instabilities. Such limitations give EMs a rather transitional feature, compromising the crucial balance needed between policymaking commitment and flexibility (Bassan, 2015). Commitment to a course of policy is desirable for attractive productive investments but may not be credible. Flexibility, on the other hand, is needed to respond to unexpected developments but may be abused. This renders rigid commitments impractical, and hence, flexibility is desirable as long as there prevails some degree of commitment that would guarantee the basic elements of governance and discipline. It is worth noting that the most favorable form of transition EMs could possible experience is the transcendence from transaction-specific orientations to institutional commitment setups. An institutionally "mature" economy that incorporates policy reform manifests itself as the right habitat for applying timely and innovative solutions at times of unexpected crises.

As most (except for Egypt and India) EMs under the scope of this study encompass resource-rich countries, the SWFs they possess may not adhere to a "one-size-fits-all" stratagem. While most of them share common features, the macroeconomic policy directions they adopt to achieve stabilization, investment, or even savings targets are customized according to each country's needs and priorities. This phenomenon could not be valid anymore with respect to resource-rich EMs. Gulf EMs in particular have received substantial praise and also skepticism in response to their ambitious diversification plans that shed newly born importance toward environment-friendly sustainable projects (WEF, 2018). For example, Saudi Arabia, UAE, and Oman all launched promising agendas – such as the Kingdom's Vision for 2030 and the UAE Vision 2030 – expanding the role of the non-hydrocarbon sector to achieve sustainable and inclusive economic growth, with measurable key performance indicators for reasons of good governance and objective monitoring. Each of these countries is aiming at endorsing the economic role of certain key sectors, such as financial services, manufacturing, tourism, and logistics among others. Almost every emerging economy has pledged to invest heavily in its logistics and transportation facilities to give a push to its touristic industry. Besides such endorsements, Emerging Gulf Markets focused on utilizing the expertise of the private sector through privatization initiatives and PPPs. Meanwhile, countries like Kuwait, Oman, Qatar, UAE, and KSA took impressive strides in reforming their used-to-be rigid investment environments, embarking on one-stop windows that nurtured bureaucracy-free investment habitats. The volatility of their oil prices presented troubling pressure, yet it fueled their drive toward supporting such initiatives. This pressure-driven stance shifted their previously reactive approaches to more proactive ones. Being resource-exporting nations, reactive policy prioritizes short-term stability in the face of surplus revenues, while proactive policy necessitates identifying a country's comparative advantages and mobilizing all available tools to capitalize on them (WEF, 2018).

This policy shift was a reflection of the best-fit strategy to effectively allocate natural resource earnings and entailed adhering to a chronological series of steps to do so. In this series, no step could be satisfactorily achieved until its predecessor was efficaciously instated. The chronology went as follows: 1. Resource-rich economies would need to embark on the accumulation of cushion reserves that mitigated the impact of probable natural resource price shocks. In other words, create stabilization SWFs that would hold assets negatively correlated with commodity prices whose earnings would be sought for at times of plunging prices, and vice versa. (Success stories that managed to mitigate the effects of natural resource curses emerged in EMs like Chile and Papua New Guinea.[22]) 2. The re-injection

---

[22] Papa New Guinea enjoyed substantial resource revenues from liquefied natural gas production and accordingly created its Mineral Resources Stabilization Fund as early as 1974. At the time, the fund had an investment strategy that combined both domestic and offshore projects. Yet, these generous investments came with a cost, which was a drop in returns of domestic assets and

of current export earnings to diversified asset portfolios that would generate guaranteed yields to future generations; and last but not least 3. The adoption of an "investing-to-invest" strategy that caters to domestic investment appetites and development priorities, country by country. Evidence from resource-rich emerging countries in the last decade has shown how the remarkable proliferation of SWFs was the one solution that optimized resource revenues in quality-investment decisions.

The impact(s) of these SWFs' investments generally overlap with intentions to address development needs and the achievement of sustainable growth. Global attention is now devoted to emerging economies and the potential of growth there. Some leading examples from the African continent have paved their way to the international scene with lots of noise. Countries like Ghana, Kenya, and Nigeria recently established their SWFs with the aim to invest domestically, regionally, as well as internationally, and hence, play an important role in global development in general (Markowitz, 2020). There are a handful of African success stories with regard to management of SWFs, especially with the ample room the latter has for further growth and expansion. A number of such success stories rely, however, on the presence of credible governance and transparency procedures and impact-assessment projects. In light of these prerequisites for successful SWFs' ventures, it is crucial to assert how the prevailing challenges in some EMs, such as those related to disclosure of information, unfortunately cost the concerned states potential inflows of investments that could otherwise have unsurmountable economic gains to society. Hence, it is evident to all how lack of transparency, particularly with respect to fiscal rules, gives rise to corruption and inefficient management of available funds and thereby impedes macroeconomic growth. With the mounting stardom SWFs are exhibiting, states are optimistic toward the somehow-novel vehicles that devise the capacity to address the challenges mentioned if they adhere to providing transparent frameworks that govern the funds' assets and investment tactics. It is not only corruption that poses as an impediment to the process, but also the absence of the rule of law, institutional development, and accountability.

---

pressure on the size and scale of the financial market. The government then decided to reorient the strategy of its sovereign fund and devote it entirely to offshore asset investments, while carefully administering the inflows into the country. This of course was to maintain minimum inflationary pressures locally, while keeping a close eye on domestic aggregate demand. The rationale was that an investment program that was externally oriented would help protect the competitiveness of the non-resource sectors of the local economy by sterilizing mineral resource revenues. The government believed that investing the proceeds offshore would give it the flexibility to invest in the domestic economy consistent with its absorptive capacity and at a rate "that does not unduly appreciate the currency or cause undue inflationary pressures."

It has been proven in literature that emerging economies that set up SWFs, particularly those who recently discovered vast supplies of natural endowments (case of Ghana in 2007), do so to create a more diversified economic platform to mitigate the risks involved in overdependence on single-commodity exports. Besides this argument, emerging SWFs seek to guarantee a stable flow of returns for both current and future generations from these earnings. Ultimately, SWFs are meant to catalyze domestic economic growth and development, alongside protecting respective sovereign states from unexpected economic shocks. However, such economic gains do not pour into the laps of sovereign owners alone, but also the host countries into which the investments flow. Hence, mutual benefits from investment partnerships between initiator and recipient (host) countries are highly recognized. Yet, despite the acknowledged benefits, a fundamental concern resides in the necessary assimilation between the visiting SWFs' objectives with that of the host country's development agenda. If fittingly articulated, guest funds have the ability to contribute to a host's development goals and hence give it immunity against the scares of inflation and appreciating exchange rates. Such articulation is to be accompanied by a properly designed balance between the targets to be achieved by the SWF and the absorptive capacity of the hosting country without jeopardizing the latter's macroeconomic stability. Such balance needs to commence with the buffering of the resource-rich country from price volatility, which represents the biggest threat to any commodity-based wealth. This buffering would involve deploying a stabilization fund that would maintain the macroeconomic steadiness needed at times of both high-resource revenue earnings and vice versa. Such steadiness addresses clear and transparent rules of deposits and withdrawals into and out of a fund, respectively, to establish the smoothing-out of government expenditures whenever necessary.

Proceeding with the deployment of a stabilization fund, the host country is advised to launch another fund with domestic development mandates that would focus on the enhancement of local industrialization and act as a guarantee for a solid base serving the country's social and economic welfare. Another function of such development SWFs is a partnering stakeholder who has the capacity to participate in investment strategies with foreign counterparts and would actually provide an element of security and safety to the latter, especially at times when accountability, governance, and political tensions pose as a threat. Such a development fund would also catalyze the initiatives of co-investments with not only foreign institutions but also the domestic private sector, and therefore, contribute directly to the investment portfolio the host country could enjoy.

7 SWFs Investments in Sustainable Development

Since the ratification of the Paris Agreement and the adoption of the SDGs, worldwide collaborative efforts have been made to enhance the promotion of investment in their related sectors. These include, but are not restricted to, infrastructure, climate change mitigation, food and agriculture, health, telecommunications, ecosystems, and biodiversity. Further efforts have also been devoted to the decision-making process and asset allocation as preliminary steps in sustainability-driven investments. These have emerged as recent attempts of ESG integration, as they also encompass updated issues of concern such as food security and education (Virgis, 2020). According to the United Nations Conference on Trade and Development (UNCTAD), 55 countries implemented almost 200 policy measures related to these sectors, with the vast majority of them aiming at liberalizing or facilitating investment. Yet, global investment in the SDGs is falling short of the target to close the US$2.5 trillion annual financing gap for developing countries (Zhan & Paulino, 2021).

The investment requirements for the SDGs were first assessed in UNCTAD's World Investment Report 2014. The report identified ten relevant sectors (encompassing all seventeen SDGs) and claimed that achieving the goals will take between US$5 and US$7 trillion, with an investment gap in developing countries of about US$2.5 trillion per year (Center for the Governance of Change, 2019). Among the world's fifty largest PPFs and thirty largest SWFs, the UNCTAD finds that only sixteen PPFs and four SWFs published a sustainable or responsible investment report in 2019 (UNCTAD, 2020).

Unfortunately, the health crisis of the COVID-19 pandemic in early 2020 exacerbated the financial constraints and led to a setback of almost six years of work (Zhan & Santos-Paulino, 2021). While the pre-COVID-19 annual financing gap for the SDGs was estimated to amount to US$ 2.5 trillion, it increased by 50 percent in 2020 and reached US$ 3.7 trillion (OECD, 2020). Currently, the financing gap exceeds by far development cooperation budgets worldwide. The crisis demonstrated how the negligence of environmental risks can expose both society and the economy to natural disasters, as well as pandemics, that can brutally devalue asset-based SWFs, destabilize their financial positions, and jeopardize their obligations to beneficiaries.

On the other side, private-sector investments in sectors related to sustainable development were also projected to drop substantially post COVID-19. Despite overall stagnant investment from both private and public sectors, the global effort to fight the pandemic somehow boosted the growth of sustainability funds, particularly social bonds and other sustainability-themed instruments. Although public funding remains the dominant source for financing sustainable goals, there is ample room for the private sector to contribute, provided there is greater clarity on invested assets and project incentives. According to Zhan and Santos-Paulino (2021), "International private investment in SDG sectors has not reached the required levels in developing countries." Despite the presence of some light at the end of the tunnel, the situation still remains dim and demands the alignment of investments with more responsible and sustainable criteria that impact the ESG practices of economic actors (UNCTAD, 2020).

There is no doubt that all SDGs are interwoven in one way or another. For example, achieving education for all (Goal 4) will have its positive spillover effect on creating decent jobs (Goal 8), which will consequently assist in attaining primary health services for the majority of those who need it (Goal 3) and will thereby lead to a healthy and thriving economy that can accommodate innovative industries and build sustainable infrastructures (Goal 9). This is just a mere demonstration of how SDGs are intricately connected and hence require an equally sophisticated and massive network of funding by diverse stakeholders who will see to their implementation. In conclusion, according to OECD, institutional investors potentially represent a major source of long-term financing to support sustainable growth in developing countries.

According to the OECD (2021), institutional investors hold trillions of dollars in AUM[23] (Hentov & Petrov, 2017). Reallocating just a small fraction of these funds to impact-driven investing opportunities has the ability to spur huge progress toward meeting the SDGs. Challenged by the setback imposed by the COVID-19 pandemic, new financing sources are needed now more than ever, particularly for both developing and emerging economies (OECD, 2021).

Despite the setbacks, and due to their extended maturity dates, SWFs are in a better position to assess long-term risks, making them more responsive to ESG- and SDG-related issues. As a matter of fact, long-term finance plays a pivotal role in fulfilling physical investment needs across all sectors of the economy, let alone environment-friendly ones. These are referred to as sustainable financial schemes. Sustainable finance is defined by IMF as the incorporation of ESG principles into business decisions, economic development, and investment strategies (Cevik & Jalles, 2020).

According to the International Forum of Sovereign Wealth Funds (2016), partakers highlighted that SWFs are particularly well positioned to become architects in green investment. The fact that the majority of the Forum's members are oil-rich countries is a driving force (for them) to reach out to

---

[23] Asset class definitions in this study are restricted to three broad categories: cash and fixed income (grouped together as it is hard to distinguish highly short-term and liquid-fixed income instruments from cash accounts); equities; and private markets – mainly real estate, alternatives, and private equity.

economic diversification of their soon-ending fossil-fuel wealth into industries that would yield "greener" and more sustainable societal, economic, and financial benefits. For example, in January 2017, UAE's capital Abu Dhabi's green investment vehicle Masdar – owned by SWF Mubadala – acquired a 25 percent stake in Hywind, a UK wind farm, following an earlier ownership increase to 80 percent in Shams Power – a world leading concentrated solar power plant. This is part of a strategy by Abu Dhabi to move away from reliance on hydrocarbons and to establish itself as a "global center of excellence in the renewable energy and clean technology sector (Braunstein, 2017).

As previously emphasized, SWFs enjoy a long-term investment spectrum and hence possess a unique advantage to promote sustainable development results. Accordingly, in December 2017, a "One Planet Summit" was held under the umbrella of assessing the SDGs attainments and subsequently, the "One Planet Sovereign Wealth Fund Working Group" was established. The coalition was founded in order to accelerate efforts to integrate financial risks and opportunities related to climate change in the management of large, long-term asset pools (OPSWF, 2018). The three main guidelines on which the OPSWF framework is based include: alignment, ownership, and integration of climate change and SDG-related risks and opportunities into investment management to improve the resilience of long-term investment portfolios. The framework was developed to accommodate countries at different levels of economic development. It also encompasses country-by-country domestic provisions, legal and regulatory requirements, and its SWFs' specific mandates. The OPSWF additionally supports its members in transitioning into more climate-oriented investment portfolios and opportunities. It achieves its objectives via initiating collaborative projects within its membership arena, particularly in financial systems that incorporate SDGs. It also assists in developing investment decision-making through improved data polling and sharing and hence enhanced identification of priority areas. The OPSWF also calls for "peer exchange" activities to improve mutual understanding of the framework's building blocks, processes, and performance indicators related to sustainable development in general and climate change in particular. In 2020, the OPSWF collaborated with IFSWF in an attempt to assess the attitude of some selected samples of SWFs toward climate change, sustainable investments, and governance issues (IFSWF, 2020b). The sample studied comprised forty-two SWFs where 81 percent (thirty-four of them) confirmed the dire need to address the financial necessity of sustainability investments, clarifying that otherwise will negatively impact economic growth and financial returns worldwide. Nevertheless, SWF owners confirmed that countries needed to also revisit their climate-related investment policies, while bearing in mind associated financial risks.

Moving beyond awareness to action, the transcendence now will involve a shift from mere climate policies to shrewd capital allocations. Unfortunately, research has shown that just over a third of currently existing SWFs confirmed having a ratified ESG strategy embedded in their SWFs investment directives. As recently as 2018, the remaining majority lacked any official or formal strategy to incorporate sustainable investment mandates. Still searching for a rewarding business case, the bulk of SWF under scrutiny still lingers in the infant stages of developing, let alone executing, their policies of environment protection. The current scene shows that the balance between awareness and actual action still strikes as uneven. Top surveyed SWFs (e.g., sampled SWFs by region included Central, South and East Asia, Oceania, North America, and North Africa) confirmed that one main challenge moving forward was the accessibility of reliable data on the expected return on investments (ROIs) on ESG-based investment projects financed entirely by SWFs. This challenge manifested itself prominently even among the most developed governments.

Referring back to the striking finding that claimed sixteen out of the world's largest fifty PPFs and four out of the top thirty SWFs published a sustainable investment report, it was only logical to assume the former had a stronger contribution to sustainability criteria relative to the latter. Ultimately, pension funds are similar to conventional savings accounts that yield monthly retirement payments to their beneficiaries. In some situations, governments form large pools of capital to finance public pension systems, that is, Public Pension Reserve Funds (PPRFs). While SWFs are set up to diversify and improve the return on excess foreign exchange reserves or commodity/non-commodity revenue mainly to shield the domestic economy from external price or supply shocks, PPFs are set up to contribute to financing pay-as-you-go pension plans (Blundell-Wignall et al., 2008). Nevertheless, according to Rempel and Gupta (2020), at least €79 billion in liquid fossil-fuel assets are localized in a tiny number of PPFs from a sample of European countries, suggesting that OECD pension funds may jointly manage between €238 and €828 billion if added to this figure. Sustainability reports reveal that pension funds engage in five actions to implement climate policies: (1) divestment, (2) direct engagement, (3) carbon footprint calculations, (4) investing in "green" alternatives, and (5) engaging in climate-oriented coalitions. However, evidence has shown that the actual implementation of these policies has rendered itself ineffective. Little has been done to mitigate the environmental hazards resulting from the investments of the PPFs in the fossil-fuel sector.

In a recent empirical study by Wurster and Schlosser (2021), an investigation was conducted to explore how a number of external variables impacted the degree to which SWFs disclosed sustainability criteria within their mandates.

The findings of this study shed light on the impact of certain SWFs characteristics on such disclosures. These characteristics included (a) the structure of the SWF (e.g., PPFs versus SWFs), (b) size of AUM, (c) source of funding, (d) economic status of the country of origin, (e) natural resource wealth of the country of origin, (f) demography of country of origin, (g) political democracy, (h) state capacity, and (i) IFSWF membership of the country of origin. It was assumed one more time that PPFs had a more profound contribution to wealth accumulation and sustainability development. Other findings were of equally interesting nature. First, a direct relationship was highlighted between the size of the AUM and the degree to which a fund was sustainable in regard to its investment appetite. Of course, the larger the AUM, the higher the chances of the fund to be interested in diversifying into more sustainable projects. Second, the source of funding and the degree of activity the fund exercises also contributes to its involvement in sustainable projects. Oil-revenue-based funds tend to cherish greater purchasing power by default, and hence are characterized by more impactful presence in the sustainable development investment arena. Third, the economic status of the country from which the fund is originating tends to determine the incentives behind its investment approaches and also its restrictive structures. Both exercise direct influence on the orientation of the fund's sustainable development profile. In other words, the economic development level of a country will determine the level of information disclosure it performs, and the expectations of its investment orientations, respectively. For instance, richer, more-developed countries are privileged with less pressure to invest toward faster and higher-return yielding projects than their less-developed counterparts. This relatively lower degree of pressure grants them the opportunity to explore more sustainably oriented ventures, especially as its citizens become more concerned with post-materialistic values (such as sustainability and future generations' welfare). Fourth, it was discovered that the natural resource wealth of a country tends to have a negative relationship with sustainable orientations among respective SWFs. For example, the greater the natural resource reserves a nation possesses, the lower the percentage of investments that get injected into sustainably viable projects. Although a rather alarming connection, this was justified by the tendency of resource-rich countries to continue investing in their current natural energy resources at the expense of protecting their environments. With substantial tempting financial returns from such investments, resource-rich countries are prone to get accused of such strategies. Hence, a hypothesis was drawn stating that the greater the natural resource wealth, the lower the sustainability investment criteria disclosed by such nations. However, evidence from other resource-based countries, particularly in the Arab Gulf states, have shown shrewd foresight of the soon-to-be depleted oil and gas reserves and have taken major strides toward more sustainable sources of fund raising.

Fifth, the demography of the country of origin of the SWF has also been proven to directly correlate with the investment orientation and disclosure of sustainable investment criteria. To further clarify this notion, it was proved that the "younger" the population, the more aware society tends to be of sustainability concerns and environment protection measures. Such awareness and concerns spring from the apprehension this young population carries toward the welfare of their own future and that of their offsprings. This hypothesis was contradicted in countries with a more inverted population pyramid, where aging societies prevail. An interesting explanation resorted to the perception that they will not be alive to witness the environmental hazards their harmful investments are creating. Such a battle was to be better fought by younger generations.

With respect to the sixth factor affecting sustainable investments and the criteria of disclosure of such investment, orientations are connected to the political environment of a nation. The degree of political democracy assumes the more democratic a political regime is in any given country of origin of an SWF, the more sustainable investments' criteria the latter discloses in its mandates. Although SWFs are said to be separated from governments and political positions of their origin countries to ensure neutral political directions, governments still have the power to influence the investment directions their SWFs may pursue. Nevertheless, strong democracies are assumed to possess strong political competition, open public participation, freedom of expression, better practices of transparency and accountability; hence, such governments are obliged to justify their actions to the general public and democratic representations. Such justification originates from the constant scrutiny governments encounter and hence expected to be more responsive to their societies' preferences, compared to their autocratic counterparts.

There is no doubt that the ability of any state to accomplish official goals set by its government depends on the right administrative skills it is expected to deploy. Such deployment is often causally related to the level of democratic empowerment prevalent in that particular state. Such democratic liberation is more often than not found in co-existence with social empowerment and higher-education attainment levels of a country, and hence more transparent disclosure of sustainable investment criteria in their SWF mandates.

A country's affiliation to international organizations and global governance entities, in this case the IFSWF, is automatically linked to the degree of inspection they will have to go through with each investment venture they decide to delegate to its SWF. Such scrutiny and adherence to best governance and sustainable investment measures somehow guarantees maximum possible disclosure of sustainable investment criteria. With such international affiliations and membership statuses, SWFs commit to the generally accepted Santiago Principles and therefore disclose more sustainable criteria into their mandates, and vice versa.

7.1 SWFs and Sustainability Investments after COVID-19

There are no doubts how global markets were severely affected by the COVID-19 pandemic in 2020. Yet, despite the downturns of the crisis, the situation gave rise to a plethora of investment opportunities for SWFs. As some SWFs entered the pandemic with substantial amounts of cash reserves, they were in a position to support their domestic economies while also taking advantage of attractive opportunities in global markets. These SWFs acted as supportive fiscal policy tools to their respective governments to mitigate the economic impact of the coronavirus and cushioned domestic sectors against setbacks, as in the case of Temasek, Singapore. Similarly, Norway's SWF made the largest contribution after its Ministry of Finance withdrew about US$37 billion from its wealth fund in 2020 to protect the economy from the dual shocks of the COVID-19 pandemic and lower crude oil prices (Sidra Capital, 2021). In 2020, the IFSWF traced investments that reached as high as US$48.6 billion in direct equity (a figure twice the size recorded in the year before), with noticeable focus on renewable energy sectors, food-security projects, logistics, e-commerce, water management, agricultural innovation, and biodiversity protection, among a few. This considerable doubling up of SWFs investments (which also represents a fourfold increase over 2016) signpost how the latter maintained their investment appetite toward risky assets as they embarked on purchasing what is referred to as "high-quality" stocks during the pandemic in order to exploit the plunging market valuations and thus "rebalance" their investment portfolios for the long term (Sidra Capital, 2021).[24]

Despite the apparent progress made in allocating funds toward investing in the SDGs, it is also crucial for countries to succeed in integrating good ESG practices in business operations to ensure positive investment impact. "Security regulators and policymakers, as well as international organizations, such as the UN Sustainable Stock Exchanges initiative and the International Organization of Securities Commissions (IOSCO), push for ESG integration in capital markets" (UNCTAD, 2021).

---

[24] According to the IFSWF in 2021, major SWFs making investments in listed equities include ADIA, Norway's Government Pension Fund Global, China Investment Corporation (CIC), Kuwait Investment Authority (KIA), and Singapore's GIC Private Limited.

To encourage the direction of SWFs toward more sustainable investments, governments need to exert and apply many efforts and reforms, respectively. For example, they will be required to provide the necessary infrastructure to support SDG-related projects. They will need to aggressively adopt and execute both policy and structural reforms that will pave the road for more business-friendly environments that will attract the right investors. There will be emphasis devoted to the private sector, considering the substantial impact the latter could have on such investments and their proliferation. Governments could actually adopt rewarding incentives in the form of potential partnerships with the private sector, which would guarantee a handful of valuable privileges, not to mention the ability to contribute with large equity capital. Such rewards could be conditional to the provision and evidence of first-class commitment to SDGs on behalf of private-sector stakeholders.

Such efforts may risk their noble objectives if no measurable SDG metrics are made available. According to UN reports, such metrics are not currently fully developed, but with the enhancements and fast-paced developments of data science and machine learning, there is hope to have them furnished soon.

According to the 2021 Annual Report published by the IFSWF, analysts agree that the halt in economic growth caused by COVID-19 was actually beneficial in some ways for the environment and that it represented a wake-up call in terms of sustainability for companies and investors alike. The One Planet SWF Group, set up in 2018 by six SWFs, attracted nine more SWFs in addition to a total of nineteen asset managers and private investment firms at the end of November 2020.[25] But is membership of such organizations enough, or is it just another form of greenwashing? Thanks to the Global SWF's GSR Scoreboard, issues of governance, sustainability, and resilience of SWFs (and PPFs) can be assessed.

8 EMs as Institutional Investors

The performance of EMs is usually put to the test at normal times, and even more so at times of disruptions. The COVID-19 pandemic was certainly a time when all markets were severely challenged by full-fledged lockdowns, and EMs were not any luckier than their developed counterparts. As the crisis embarked on its second year in 2021, some EMs proved more agile and resilient than others, depending on their macroeconomic policies and how they were administered. Some adopted unprecedented rescue packages to their more vulnerable sectors, while others were cushioned on reservoirs of funds that were injected into the economic system to mitigate economic downturns. After stressful

---

[25] Of the 3,575 signatory members of UNPRI today, over a quarter signed up in 2020.

periods of financial bottlenecks, most EMs managed to re-surface into the scene, with a handful of innovative and unconventional debt-management tools to meet their financing needs.[26] However, with the entire world struggling to recover – some at a different pace than others – uncertainty and market volatility were nothing short of inevitable. There is no doubt that different recoveries in EMs echoed dissimilarities in economic positions and policy approaches. Those that were able to contain the virus and impose strict measures to endorse mass vaccinations (such as the UAE) achieved faster recoveries. Those with ample fiscal buffers, market access, or both were able to deploy greater fiscal support (such as Saudi Arabia and Ghana). In some countries, the credibility of central banks paved the way for cuts in interest rates to first-time lows and engaged in unconventional monetary policy without severe exchange rate pressure (Fratto et al., 2021). Yet, EMs with macroeconomic imbalances or substantial debt burdens continue to face sharp trade-offs between supporting recovery and reducing imbalances (as in the case of Egypt). Despite the differing contexts, SWFs emerged as critical reconstruction tools at the time of the crisis.

As SWFs showcased a rapid increase in emerging economies since 2000 (Kalter & Schena, 2013), attention was directed toward them and the role everyone expected them to play.

Unfortunately, the significant uncertainty in the global economy (triggered by the health crisis) had its toll on the investment landscape worldwide, particularly on institutional investors, which at the time, managed more than US$8 trillion as AUM. As a result, the tactics of SWFs shifted in response to the global economic and geopolitical dynamics. EMs with large cash reserves held in their oil-based SWFs were capable of investing into their domestic economies and also worked hard to allure potential investors into their local markets to spur further economic activity and recovery. Meanwhile, worldwide SWFs were showing more interest in alternative investment channels such as private equity and other high-return yielding assets in an attempt to abandon lower returns in other more conventional ones such as sovereign bonds. Accordingly, EMs stood as potential and lucrative environments, ready to absorb such investments. With all the dynamics around EMs, whether as large SWF owners or investment

---

[26] Economic relief measures included expansionary approached to fiscal policies that encompassed increases in government spending. Monetary policy encountered similar approaches where liquidity measures were offered to firms and banks while ease of credit was also witnessed. Low domestic inflation and monetary easing by advanced economies also gave central banks in EMs room to cut domestic policy rates substantially. Household savings increased in most EMs following the onset of the pandemic. Much of the domestic savings went to finance the government, reducing the need for foreign borrowing, which, together with lower private investment, kept current account deficits in check (IMF, 2021).

destinations, a selected sample of cases in the upcoming section serves as an attempt to explore how they stood, and still do, in face of multiple challenges.

Yet, the question of entering emerging economies relates to a key challenge of getting the right internal culture to invest in a meaningful way (Sharma, 2017). Putting this challenge aside, the impact of SWFs on recipient countries of the emerging world is another spectrum altogether.

A central question in the SWF literature is whether SWFs improve or deteriorate the performance of their target recipients. From one perspective, SWFs as large institutional investors entering EMs can actually offer financial sustenance and also expansion opportunities for their host counterparts. However, they are presumed to inflict negative spillovers on the financial performance and governance practices by pursuing noncommercial objectives (Garg & Shukla, 2021a).

In the past, common impediments to increasing volumes of SWFs in EMs were due to lack of conviction from the general public, cultural issues, and currency-related risks. In addition to these impediments, obtaining the right benchmarks for EM investments was challenging due to the lack of depth in capital markets. However, an increasing number of emerging countries have been establishing Natural Resource Funds (NRFs) – *sovereign funds financed by natural resource wealth* – to regulate the flow of resource-related capital in the economy. Of the fifty-two NRFs recorded in 2019 alone, thirty-one (60 percent) were established since 2000 (Ghosh, 2019). The remarkable interest sprang from the intention of EMs to enhance the external stability of their respective home economies, allocating privatization proceeds to these investment vehicles to protect the rights of future generations in benefiting from them rather than directing such proceeds to finance current government expenditure and budget deficits (Elbaz, 2018). As SWFs are characterized by their agility and dynamism in setting up their mandates, they have been enthusiastically adopted by rising economies new to the scene where they gracefully mapped their respective development agendas and objectives to the latter. In this regard, SWFs are institutions largely created by and exploited for the benefit of emerging economies, that is, they are emerging market institutions (Kalter & Schena, 2013). From a macroeconomic perspective, the rapid accumulation of assets under management across EMs and their respective SWFs could only be assessed as a positive outcome if and only if the absorptive capacity of the domestic economy was accommodative enough to permit the investment of these assets locally. As the nature of this so-called absorptive capacity develops over time rather than all of a sudden, there is a dire need to shrewdly manage surging AUMs to re-inject them into the local economy in the most efficient manner without triggering spillover effects such as the Dutch disease.

According to Sharma (2017), despite the identified challenges, there are a number of global dynamics that would suggest EMs as attractive destinations for reliable long-term capital. Two of the most recognized advantages of investing in emerging economies are (1) the potential for growth and (2) diversification of economic portfolio. Nevertheless, regulations and guidelines are important drivers of ESG integration by public pension and SWFs, even in the context of EMs. In other words, their diversification and growth potential will not overshadow the necessity of such regulations.

In 2020, the UNCTAD identified the three main categories of such regulations and guidelines as follows: (1) government regulations, (2) stewardship codes,[27] and (3) international guiding principles. Although most of them are voluntary, PPFs and SWFs are taking them into account in their ESG integration activities (Engel et al., 2020).

This section sheds light on a selected sample of EMs and their respective SWFs.[28] Selection of the countries was based on the region they originated from (Kingdom of Saudi Arabia and the UAE representing the GCC region; Egypt and Ghana representing the African continent; while India providing the Asian flavor). Another criterion for selecting this specific country mix goes back to the dynamic and often fascinating backgrounds they offer. For example, the latest investment profile of Saudi Arabia's Public Investment Fund (PIF) showed accelerating activity like never before. The PIF succeeded in diversifying its investment portfolio too much that it is now delving into unconventional channels such as entertainment and social media. The Kingdom is known to be transforming itself into a rapidly changing ecosystem, with huge developments in its economic, financial, and even social landscapes. The road map of these changes is embedded in its 2030 Vision drafted in 2016, and there is strong evidence that the country's SWF is the engine behind accomplishing them. With all these dynamic activities taking place, it is easy to assume the PIF and the Kingdom may offer many lessons to be learned, hence are worth the examination.

On the other hand, its UAE counterpart from the same region managed to jump a handful of ranks across Governance indexes, raising questions of why this was not done any earlier.

With respect to Ghana, the country was one of the prominent examples of those who embarked on recent natural resource discoveries and hence were relatively new entrants to the game. Every decision Ghana took at the time of

---

[27] Typically, the stewardship codes focus on governance issues such as conflict of interest, voting, monitoring, and engaging with investees, and disclosure of relevant policies and practices.

[28] In the case of the UAE, only two SWFs were included in this study: Mubadala and ADIA. Other SWFs were not selected due to the absence of sufficient information needed to adequately present their case.

establishing its first SWF was observed with skepticism, simply because it was subconsciously judged on how it will outperform its counterparts and learn from its predecessors' mistakes.

Egypt, on the other hand, was specifically selected because of the unique structure of the assets it possessed under its management, and on which it founded its first SWF. With the radical economic structural reforms it adopted back in 2016,[29] Egypt led an innovative approach to launch its first-time SWF, aiming to maximize economic and financial benefits from under-utilized government-owned assets and inviting the private sector to join their aim. The Sovereign Fund of Egypt (TSFE) is considered a development-strategic Fund, and like many of its counterparts, was set up without much "wealth." It is considered an interesting case to study, especially with its attempts to catalyze foreign capital and fundraise debt and equity from other state-owned investments (IFSWF, 2021d).

Finally, India represents an interesting case as it was the only BRICS country that did not own an SWF until 2015. Once it did so, it emerged as an attractive destination for many offshore SWF investments due to its promising growth momentum. One more reason worth exploring India's journey in the world of SWFs is its relatively stable political environment and healthy appetite for structural reform; all ingredients for a successful relationship between its own SWFs and those it is to host.[30] Furthermore, the IMF predicted striking growth figures for the country in 2021, stating how its drive toward state-of-the-art transformations in the digital arena and its blossoming manufacturing base could crown its strong comeback.

Background, governance structures, and investments into sustainable development are key criteria for exploration across the selected countries and their respective SWFs. Ultimately, every country demonstrates a unique and stand-alone model that can be showcased to the world.

8.1 SWFs in the Kingdom of Saudi Arabia as an EM

Saudi Arabia's commodity-based SWF (known as the PIF) was founded in 1971 with the objective to invest solely in domestic sectors and finance domestic commercial projects. Today, its current share of international investments amounts to 20 percent of its portfolio. The impressive transition from a

---

[29] Egypt committed to a program of economic structural reform advised by the IMF when it was granted a substantial amount of financial aid at the time. One of the first steps Egypt took toward such reform was the free-floating of its Egyptian pound against the US dollar, and other countries. This led to an immediate depreciation of the pound and severe hikes in inflation and trade balance deficits.

[30] In 2020, offshore SWFs invested a record US$14.8 billion in India.

local-based SWF to an international one was endorsed by the country's private sector empowering policies,[31] accumulated oil wealth, and ambitious leadership.

The PIF is considered the Kingdom's pivotal role-player in achieving its 2030 vision and a leading economic catalyst. Selected as the SWF of the Year in 2020 by the IFSWF,[32] PIF's main sources of funding include capital injections from the government, state assets transferred to the PIF, loans and debt instruments, and retained earnings from investments (McPherson-Smith, 2021). Other Fund assets include sector development projects, real estate, and most notably, the so-called giga projects that target huge deserted plots of land only to turn them to full-fledged ecosystems, as in the case of the two Red Sea projects, Neom and Qiddiya (which translate to "new future").

The PIF's offshore portfolio includes a rather diversified pool of liquid direct and indirect investments spread across private equity, real estate, public equity, and also debt assets.

Today, PIF is considered one of the top-tier SWFs in the world. Such success was embodied by the Kingdom's active membership with the G20, taking strides in strategic investment operations, acquisition deals, infrastructure, and establishing key partnerships. These significant achievements came to resonate with Vision 2030's mission, programs and initiatives to spark a change fueled by a robust, reliable, and stable economic arm. Currently, the PIF's mandate is to lead the way for the Kingdom's diversification road map, while minimizing its dependence on oil. The Fund is ambitiously aiming to be the largest in the world, with AUM to reach US$2 trillion by 2030.

Governance Framework

In 2015, the PIF justified its expansionary moves as politically driven. Yet, in the years following that announcement, the Fund explicitly declared its economic motives to serve its country as both a stabilization and development fund. The Fund also disclosed its intention to achieve economic diversification and endorse the presence of its private sector while attracting foreign direct investments (FDIs). Emphasis was devoted to knowledge and technology sharing and transfer, respectively. From a governance perspective, the PIF is known for its limited commitment to transparency, especially with respect to the integration of its finances into the government's fiscal policy. According to the IFSWF and

---

[31] These included amended regulations that called for more public–private partnerships, and business-friendly initiatives to encourage the proliferation of the private sector as a driving force of economic growth. This gave more room for the PIF to divert its attention toward international investment opportunities.

[32] Announced in the 2021 Annual report released by the IFSWF.

the latest L-M Transparency Index, the PIF scored 6/10 as of September 2021. Despite such claims, the Fund insists on disclosing the opposite stance by confirming its adherence to governance best practices and universally accepted transparency procedures. This pertains to its reporting and management hierarchy frameworks. For instance, at the institutional level, the PIF reports directly to the "Council of Economic and Development Affairs" and asserts that it is identified as a public legal entity with absolute financial and administrative autonomy. The obvious contradiction in judgments remains unresolved. According to Truman's SWF Scorecard, in 2019, the PIF scores 39 out of a 100.[33] Alongside transparency concerns, it has been also reported that the Fund's investment strategies have resulted in crowding out the private sector, despite its intentions to do the exact opposite (Maire et al., 2021b).

Today, and according to its latest annual reports published on its website, the Fund confirms that all its investment decisions are based exclusively on commercial grounds. Furthermore, any new investment outreach is reviewed by five different committees specialized in audit and compliance, risk assessment, talent acquisition, and strategic planning. All five key committees collaborate to guide investment. Without a doubt, the Fund's performance surpassed everyone's expectations primarily due to its apparent interest in sustainable investing and ESG. Although improvements could have risen earlier, still the establishment of its own ESG team was a step worth praising.

Investing in SDG Projects

PIF plays a vital role in achieving Saudi Arabia's dream of economic diversification and future resilience. As the Kingdom's primary investment arm, PIF collaborates with top-tier international investment entities to obtain tremendous financial returns and long-term stable value. According to its annual published reports, in 2021, the Fund showcased remarkable milestones since its inception in August of 1971, yet the most outstanding were those aligned with its Vision 2030. Some of the PIF's most boasted-about projects include, yet are not restricted to:

(1) Neom (which means "new future") is a region in northwest the country overlooking the Red Sea and is destined to be a hub for innovation and creativity across multiple sectors yet in pure sustainable terms.

---

[33] The SWF scoreboard has thirty-three elements. Each element is scored from 0 to 1, with partial scores in quarters for some elements. The total is then expressed as a percentage of 33, resulting in a scale of zero to 100. In 2019, the best performers among GCC funds were the Mubadala investment Company of the UAE, with a score of 77, and the Kuwait Investment Authority (KIA), with a score of 70. Until the latest scoreboard, the KIA had been the highest-scoring SWF in the GCC.

(2) The Red Sea Development company, also a Red-Sea-based project expected to lead the Kingdom into a new global position in the world of tourism.

(3) Qiddiya Investment Company, launched in 2018, this project aims to manifest itself as the Kingdom's Giga project, attracting the world of entertainment, sports, and arts to the Kingdom.

The Fund's most recent track record documented its cumulative AUM by the end of 2020 as approximately SAR 1.5 trillion (between US\$3.2 and US\$3.5 billion).

8.2 SWFs in the UAE as an EM

In 2007, the UAE, and in particular the capital's Investment Authority (ADIA) recorded a value of US\$875 billion in AUM. Back then, it was the wealthiest among oil-rich countries. Despite claims that the Fund does not disclose its details with utmost clarity, up-to-date revelations confirm that the fund is highly diversified in both private and global co-investments (Alsweilem et al., 2015). In the IFSWF's 2022 rankings, ADIA came third place in terms of AUM that stood at US\$ 829 billion (after Norway as 1st and China 2nd).

At the time of establishment, it was common for the country to inject its oil-reserve surpluses in more conventional channels such as gold and short-term credit assets. With time, the mandate of the Council shifted toward domestic and regional investments in a much more dynamic portfolio. For example, ADIA possesses 100 percent of shares of the capital's leading national airline company, Etihad Airways. Other significant sovereign funds in Abu Dhabi include "Mubadala" Development Company:[34] established in 2002 (referred to as "Mubadala" for short). The SWF labels itself as a sovereign investor managing diverse portfolio of assets domestically and abroad. In 2022, IFSWF ranked it as 13th in terms of AUM that stood at US\$ 243 billion. Mubadala publically positions itself as a commercially oriented entity with widespread presence across multiple geographic regions. Mubadala is not the only UAE SWF that adopts responsible investing strategies that encompass ESG principles. Its mandate clearly asserts its inclination to contribute to a more sustainable future while unlocking incremental value from its investments, by seasoning timely opportunities and mitigating risks over time.

As an EM itself, UAE expressed high interest in investing in other similar ecosystems via its own SWFs. The UAE's SOEs raced to invest in new sectors, including those of healthcare, technology, retail, and consumer, and of course,

---

[34] It later changed its name to be Mubadala Investment Company.

renewable energy. Investments in these sectors involved heavy collaboration with venture capitalists. Besides partnering with the private sector, both Mubadala and ADIA diversified their public holdings and stretched out to new Asian Markets in the region. In 2021, the IFSWF recognized Mubadala as the "Fund of the Year" based on its active partnerships deals and contribution to domestic economic recovery post the COVID-19 pandemic. It also emerged as one of the most active SWFs to seal collaborations with governments around the world.

Governance Framework

With respect to its governance framework, and particularly transparency, the IFSWF recorded the latest L-M Transparency Index for ADIA, which stood at a score of 6/10 as of September 2021. In terms of the GSR Scoreboard, the 2021 results published by the IFSWF showed a drop of two points due to its increasingly opaque annual report that did not provide a detailed organizational chart nor did it clarify the role of the government in managing the fund.

To date, ADIA is managed by a board comprised of nine executive directors of which half of them belong to the country's ruling royal blood. The emirate's prince acts as chair of its board while its managing director is the key decision-maker in matters of investments and day-to-day operations. An investment committee advises the managing director on investment policy and external manager selection and performance (around 75 percent of ADIA's assets are managed externally).[35]

Although official records state that its inauguration dates to 1976 by royal decree, yet its origins could be traced as far back as the 1960s, prior to the country's declaration of independence from British colonialism.

ADIA's mandate was always described as rather conservative, favoring sovereign debt tools of the world's leading reserve currencies. During the last decade of the twentieth century, the Fund increased its risk appetite and began seeking more diversified portfolios with greater return-potential. Despite the diversification, ADIA is still recognized as an inter-generational savings fund. The other most significant supplementary sovereign funds in Abu Dhabi, Mubadala Development Company, had better performance of governance attributed to it compared to its counterparts. It managed to score a 10 on the L-M Transparency Index as of September 2021.

---

[35] The law establishing ADIA creates a separation of roles and responsibilities among the owner (the Abu Dhabi government), the governing body and the management – the latter two bodies are involved with the institutional governance of ADIA.

Cash deposits and withdrawals into and out of the fund do not adhere to any disclosed rule; let alone formula. Nevertheless, the law requires the fund to furnish reserves available for withdrawal upon request; however, such extractions occur irregularly and records have shown that they only ever took place at times of record-low oil prices and revenues.[36]

Investing in SDG Projects

Mubadala[37] is a state investment entity that was originally inaugurated in 2002 with a mandate focusing on diversifying the country's financial returns (Lessambo, 2021). UAE SWFs have given special interest to renewable energy projects in the past few years. For example, Mubadala drafted its own "Responsible Investing Policy," which sits on the following principles: (1) incorporating ESG-related issues and their impact on financial returns, society, and the environment in capital investment decisions; (2) collaborate with partners that adopt the same ESG principles and would help it improve its overall ESG performance and impact; (3) support adequate disclosure of information related to ESG practices by partners; and (4) base its ESG investment decisions on rigorous analysis based on industry trends and futuristic scenarios. Mubadala also expanded the scope and scale of its partnerships, including collaborations with Schneider Electric[38] in sustainability-related areas and with Italy's Snam to promote hydrogen development in the UAE. As a matter of fact, ESG standards are at the heart of investment strategies of SWFs in the UAE as they strive to inject their funds both domestically and abroad, with particular emphasis in the Middle East and North African region. Toward the end of 2020, Mubadala was admitted as a full-fledged member of the IFSWF, hence adhering to the forum's Santiago Principles of governance and best practices. Most recent investment initiatives revolved around aerospace, ICT, semiconductors, metals and mining, renewable energy, oil and gas, petrochemicals, utilities, healthcare, real estate, pharmaceuticals and medical

---

[36] Since 2008, ADIA has released much more information about its mandate, objectives, and investment strategy. Such information included the publication of an annual report (without detailed financial statements or portfolio details), a dedicated ADIA website, a clarification of its external and internal governance framework, broad asset-class allocation ranges, and selected benchmarks.

[37] Mubadala is a sovereign investor managing a diverse portfolio of assets in the UAE and abroad, to generate sustainable financial returns for its shareholder, the Government of Abu Dhabi. It was established in 2017 when then-named Mubadala Development Company (now Mamoura Diversified Global Holding) and the International Petroleum Investment Company (IPIC) merged.

[38] A global company leading the Digital Transformation of Energy Management and Automation. Operates in 100 countries, Schneider is a leader in Power Management and provides integrated efficiency solutions, combining energy, automation, and software.

technology, agribusiness, and a global portfolio of financial holdings across all asset classes (IFSWF, 2020a)

8.3 SWFs in Ghana as an EM

The past two decades witnessed conspicuous changes in the geographic distribution and proliferation of SWFs across the world. The African continent specifically became a focal point, both in establishing and creating funds from new SOIs. However, these newly created African funds are certainly different from resource-rich funds that made up the early wave of their peers.

Generally, the creation of SWFs in Africa emerged hand in hand with serious attempts to attract FDIs. Such attempts aim to achieve economic growth and the development of state-of-the-art industries. With the purpose of increasing job opportunities and sustainable development, SWFs in the African continent have sought unconventional and innovative models to manage their assets. Despite the ambitious targets, achievement does not come without encountering challenging impediments.

Nevertheless, there is a handful of African success stories in regard to management of SWFs, especially with the ample room the latter has for further growth and expansion. A number of such success stories rely on the presence of credible governance and transparency procedures, and impact-assessment projects.

In the case of Ghana, petroleum-based SWFs were created in 2011. In 2007, natural resources were discovered and prior to extraction, mandates were already enacted. The result was the creation of Ghana's Stabilization Fund and Heritage Fund (that was later called Ghana's Savings Fund, GSF). Both funds aimed to achieve sustainable development in the country together with domestic development. However, the initial objectives revolved around smoothing government expenditures at times of expansionary dictates and mitigating the supply shocks resulting from volatile resource prices that affected export earnings (IFSWF, 2021a). In 2017, another fund was established, the Ghana Investment Infrastructure Fund (GIIF). The Fund's mandates are to mobilize and manage financial resources for investment in a diversified spectrum of infrastructure projects in the country, for the purposes of domestic development, urbanization, and overall industrial growth (Ministry of Finance, Ghana, 2017).

Governance Framework

Strict adherence to the Santiago Principles and overall governance protocols were pledged and the Ghana's Central Bank, alongside the Ministry of Finance, were assigned as the regulating and auditing entities for the Funds. Consequently, a "Public Investments Accounts" committee comprising all sectors of the nation's public was established to ensure the fair representation and participation of all people (Arinze-Umobi & Ihedirionye, 2021). According to the GSR Scoreboard of 2021, Ghana's GSF was an example of good transparency and a well-functioning fund yet had considerable homework to do on the ESG side.

Such structure ensured accountability measures across all three entities, together with occasional assistance from international advisories such as Norway, which also offered consultancy services to Ghana (Stone & Truman, 2016). All these elements helped the Ghana government establish clear-cut rules regarding withdrawals, monitoring, and regulation of their SWFs.

Ghana is just an example amid many African and resource-rich countries that try to shrewdly administer what is known as the natural resource curse. The discovery of natural resources should be a blessing for a country's national growth and development prospects. Paradoxically, the so-called resource curse is a phenomenon where large natural resource endowments often correlate with lower-than-expected economic growth as well as weaker, more authoritarian institutional development (Markowitz, 2020). Also known as the Dutch disease, rapidly growing export earnings from natural resources increase the demand for a national currency and cause its appreciation. This jeopardizes other export-potential sectors as it causes a rise in prices of national products and compromises their international competitiveness. Numerous policy recommendations have been devised to combat the Dutch disease or at least mitigate its spillovers. However, drafting policy solutions that are realistically executable – given the brittle institutional networks and frail public financial management structures in most developing countries, poses a critical challenge to be yet addressed.

Along with its African counterparts, Ghana's SWFs face stereotypes that place it in a position associated with risky, exotic, and mostly humanitarian investments (IFSWF, 2021d). In 2021, the IFSWF recorded a total of US$97m as AUM in Ghana's Petroleum Funds and US$330 m in its GIIF, respectively. It is important to highlight that the GIIF was actually created out of the Petroleum Funds, yet the latter is often regarded as the country's main SWF. As a matter of fact, the GIIF is also recognized to possess the upper hand in influencing its nation's economic transformation. Ironically, the figures mentioned earlier solidify the notion that the country lacks local capital financing. However, according to economic outlooks, market niches for foreign capital are abundant. Despite being known as a relatively new entrant to the SWF arena, Ghana is also known to be a well-established producer and exporter of cocoa and gold, and hence has the potential to unleash its economic diversification powers and depend less on its recently discovered oil revenues that fund its SWFs.

In 2018, a diversified international Advisory Firm based in Ghana and known as Konfidants,[39] released an SWF Index[40] encompassing twelve African countries. Known as The African Sovereign Wealth Funds Index, it is designed around seven main indicators, namely: (1) governance and public disclosure, (2) size of fund, (3) domestic investment mandate, (4) source of funding (diversification of sources), (5) financial performance, (6) economic impact, and (7) sustainability. Also referred to as the Firm's Maiden Index, its theme was "relevance." In other words, it tackled the question of "how relevant were African SWFs, as structured back then, to the continent's and its countries' development needs?" According to the 2018 Index and its seven main pillars, Nigeria, Rwanda, and Ghana[41] were the continent's best-performing funds, recording rather high and equally impressive scores in Governance & Disclosure, Size and Investment Mandate. With respect to the Governance and Public Disclosure indicator, the top five funds were Bostwana, Nigeria, Rwanda, Ghana,[42] and Angola – being the only funds that had publicly disclosed and provided accessible periodic annual audited reports since their establishment. Seven of the twelve examined SWFs declared they had Domestic Investment Mandates (the third indicator of the Index); yet only four of the seven (Angola, Morocco, Ghana, Senegal) proved to have actually invested within their domestic economies. Eight out of the twelve funds were identified as predominantly financed by oil revenue. Funds exclusively dependent on natural resource revenue included Ghana, yet it was also recognized as one of those countries that managed to establish other sources of income for itself, that is, achieved some degree of economic diversification.

From a counter perspective, Ghana, along with other African nations, has managed to attract substantial foreign SWFs investments into its territories. As far back as 2008, prominent SWFs, such as those of Norway, China, and Dubai,

---

[39] Konfidants is made up of a group of thought-leading conveners and advisors of high-impact multi-country partnerships seeking to transform Africa and drive the global emergence of African corporates. The Firm works across four main practice areas: Research & Analytics Strategy & Advisory Implementation & Project Management Convening & managing multi-country partnerships & platforms.

[40] Financial data for the African Sovereign Wealth Funds were obtained from the 2016/2017 end-of-year annual reports, or when unavailable, from the most recent year of reporting. The rankings do not therefore reflect any changes in size of the funds as may be reported starting January 2018.

[41] Ghana ranked third in the first edition of the African Sovereign Wealth Fund Index polling 62 out of 100 %. Nigeria and Rwanda scored 62.49 % and 62.24 %, respectively.

[42] Its SWF recorded a 2.05% of its GDP in 2018, and was identified as one of four most transparent funds on the continent according to the African SWF 2018 Index.

created joint development and investment funds in the continent in attempts to exploit the continent's wealth comprised of its large youthful population, abundance of natural resources, EMs' traits, and growing middle-class segments. These characteristics manifested themselves as lucrative opportunities for foreign investors (Triki & Faye, 2011). Despite these alluring features, Africa's share in foreign SWFs investments remains negligible. During the early rise of African SWF, and in 2010, Africa as a continent recorded a 5 percent attracted SWFs investment. The top three countries that hosted a mere 1.74 percent of Western SWFs resources resided mainly in South Africa, Egypt, and Morocco. At the time, tracking down the accurate volume(s) of foreign SWFs investments into Africa was cumbersome given the limitations of transparency and accessibility of information. Yet from a generic standpoint, the sectors that attracted the bulk of these investments were as follows: (1) real estate, (2) hospitality, (3) banking, (4) infrastructure, and (5) financial services.

Investing in SDG Projects

In 2017, Ghana embarked on a serious journey to deploy its SWFs toward achieving the SDGs. While focusing on particular targets that were considered more important than others, it did so in collaboration with its growing private sector, in an attempt to take advantage of its competence and agility. For illustration, the GIIF (established in 2014) injected US$51 million to a public–private partnership with a local telecommunication corporation (Broadspectrum) to develop and upgrade its domestic broadband network as a way to increase internet speed services. The project was named "the Western Corridor Project" and was recorded to create an estimated figure of 12,000 job opportunities during its initial construction phase alone (IFSWF, 2021d). This project was considered a multipurpose one as it fed into a variety of related industries such as education, infrastructure development and modernization, oil, and gas operations. Although it was led by a private-sector company, the GIIF[43] had a pivotal role in mooring the project as it identified the investment gaps hindering the telecommunications industry. It thus endowed the required funding and ensured the actual establishment and procurement of the project.

When the pandemic hit in 2020, Ghana was faced with a conundrum like no before. Just like some of its neighboring nations (Angola, Botswana, and Nigeria) Ghana had to stop at a crossroad to reassess the way it was to manage its stabilization and savings SWFs. Withdrawals were inevitable and public

---

[43] GIIF has an US$85 million facility from the French Development Agency (AFD) for on-lending to eligible projects in Ghana to help facilitate broader development across the country.

spending was ranked as a top priority for the country. Despite the presence of ongoing work on newly drafted investment strategies, Ghana knew that new allocations were certain, and new starting points were drawn accordingly. There were incidents where cash withdrawals did not affect asset allocations, yet rebalancing the portfolio was a must. The pandemic and the withdrawals it brought along with it raised flags on the Funds and their governance protocols. New outlooks for the Funds' projected inflows and risk appetites were also revised, ensuring more low-risk securities. Considerations of entering new EMs and widening portfolios of returns were explored by Ghana and other African states. Collaborations with the private sector and China in particular were at the forefront of Ghana's talks.

Unfortunately, evidence has shown that there is prominent absence of literature on the role of African SWFs in achieving the SDGs. This is a surprising observation, given the fact that the latter are actually strategic stakeholders in implementing the goals through a wide spectrum of projects such as infrastructure development, climate-conscious financing, and socially responsible investing (SRI) (Chen, 2019). Chen's study went on to forecast that if Global SWFs allocated a mere 1.3 percent of their total AUM to the African continent, it would succeed in narrowing the financial gap needed for infrastructure projects. Such a projection demonstrates the financial capacity of SWFs in addressing the issue, if so desired. Although the larger share of infrastructure investments in Africa belongs to foreign stakeholders, yet the growing size of the continent's SWFs could to a great extent surpass that share and furnish powerful results in fulfilling the needs of African nations.

Along with Morocco, Senegal, and Nigeria, Ghana is one of the many African countries that has positioned its SWFs as catalysts for climate-conscious finance and green investing. The country has allocated its SWFs reserves to enhance its capacity for renewable energy production and clean technology in an attempt to set an example to potential co-investors and private-sector stakeholders and attract them into fruitful collaborations.

Up to the point of this study, it is evident that the SWFs examined in the African context are challenged by risk and governance concerns. To mitigate these negative stereotypes, they seek to improve their credibility rankings and attract FDIs into a promising emerging market. Such attractions pertain to the continent's structural and demographic strengths. The previous regimes resorted to the provision of credit facilities and/or tax incentives for projects, yet were still challenged by corruption indicators and risk analyses. Nevertheless, it is inevitable for Ghana's SWFs to reconsider its governance frameworks and ensure the smooth alignment between its macroeconomic policies (be it fiscal or monetary) to enable long-term strategies to encompass the SDGs and pave the way for a trouble-free transition to a low-carbon economy.

8.4 The Egyptian Sovereign Wealth Fund

Egypt's SWF was officially created in 2018, and its articles of association were ratified the following year. The Fund's mandate is to contribute to the sustainable economic development of Egypt by managing its "un-utilized" assets to maximize their value for future generations, hence its main focus is internal domestic investment. Its board of directors is chaired by the Ministry of Planning and Economic Development. It is also comprised of four sub-funds that tackle crucial sectors that Egypt's 2030 Vision has prioritized. These sub-funds are classified according to their industry of focus: (1) sub-fund for utilities and infrastructure, (2) sub-fund for tourism, real estate and antiquities, (3) healthcare services sub-fund, and (4) the financial services and digital transformation sub-fund. According to the Fund's official portal, the Prime Ministerial Decree calling for the establishment of the Fund is based on the objective of "Contributing to sustainable economic development by managing its money and assets and achieving optimal utilization of them according to the best international standards and rules, to maximize their value for the sake of future generations, and for the sake of that, the Egypt's sovereign wealth fund has the right to cooperate and participate with Arab and foreign counterpart funds and various financial institutions."

The Fund intends to target strategic commercial partnerships with other sovereign funds and financial institutions to fulfill its mandate consistent with best practices with regard to environmental and social responsibility and rules of governance (IFSWF, 2020a). During the establishment phase, the Fund was recognized as an entity with unique rights and attributes, unlike traditional commercial entities. To start with, the Fund's AUM were transferred to its possession and full ownership by provision of law[44]; and these assets included unused lands, real estates, as well as a few historical assets (buildings) along with any other fixed asset that was not optimally utilized within the last ten years. In summary, TSFE had the right to acquire all plots of public land rendered redundant, and this was an unprecedented model that never existed before. For reasons of governance and effective assessment of the Fund's progress, all acquired public lands and assets are to be evaluated at market

---

[44] TSFE has authority and legislative power by law to acquire any of the unused or exploited state-owned assets and the ownership of this land will be granted by law, while also granting them the right to buy, sell, rent, lease, exploit, and benefit from the assets in terms of commercial investment management. TSFE became a full member of IFSWF in May 2022.

value before and after the acquisition. In other words, a comparison is to be made between the previous market price under fragmented ownership and afterward.

Other AUM belonging to the Fund include: (1) the fund's capital, which comprised of 5 billion Egyptian pounds at time of induction, (2) returns from investing its money and exploiting its assets, (3) loans and facilities it obtains and proceeds from issuing bonds and other financial instruments, and (4) other resources that the board of directors approves case by case, and a decision is issued by the prime minister on its acceptance (Wafi, 2021).

In 2020, TSFE accelerated its implementation steps to more than just preparatory or legal steps. By mid-year 2021, the Fund's activities became more prominent and widely heard. The fund's assets were estimated at US$ 11.959 billion according to official sources and the IFSWF.[45]

Governance Framework

As an associate member of the IFSWF, there comes some unique attributes. This form of IFSWF membership is specifically for entities that are still in their infancy stages of establishment. As an associate, TSFE has the right to voluntarily adhere to the Santiago Principles with respect to issues of governance, public information disclosure, investment decisions, and risk administration of AUM. Such membership status is granted for up to three years only from the IFSWF. As the first SWF to be established in the country, its main focus is devoted to domestic investments. Particular emphasis is given to better utilization of existing assets (such as old ministry premises, public service centers, and the like); companies, and state-of-the art fields of technology such as digital transformation and Fintech. The Fund's business model is based on acquiring assets and stakes in companies at their market value (including fixed assets) and partnering with private investors to develop, modernize, or even renew them to generate returns. Operations of TSFE occur under "sub-funds," each specialized in a specific industry and sector.

The Fund is cushioned on the government's autonomy in case any impediments may arise in front of investors and is guided by its objectives when it comes to decisions of asset mobilization. Prior to the establishment of TSFE, the Egyptian government managed to raise its competitiveness index rankings, particularly with respect to business-friendly indicators that make it an attractive destination for any FDIs and equal to its worldwide counterparts.

---

[45] The data of total current assets for TSFE obtained from the Sovereign Wealth Fund Institute published data: www.swfinstitute.org (last reported on February 14, 2021).

Along with the Egyptian government's support, The Egyptian SWF is independently managed through senior executives from the private sector. Its business model explained earlier is meant to promote the role and presence of the private sectors in the economy and increase job opportunities for Egypt's young population. The Fund's real impact resides in its capacity to identify investment channels and unique assets for investors. It aims to assist the government in implementing structural reforms and achieve economic diversification. The Fund is overseen by a board of directors as well as a general assembly, both bodies having majority private-sector members. Despite its efforts and promises to adhere to the best governance practices, TSFE scored a humble 4/10 on L–M Transparency Index as of September 2021. According to the 2021 GSR Scoreboard, TSFE needs to establish a more robust governance structure if it were to attract foreign capital investments to partner with her.

Investing in SDG Projects

TSFE has embarked on multiple projects that seek to fulfill its country's SDGs achievement agenda. Among some of the prominent ones were those instated with the UAE, as well as other domestic and foreign investors across several sustainable sectors. In late 2021, Abu Dhabi Investments Holding Company (ADQ) finalized a three-year-long deal to find a new office in Egypt's capital in an attempt to fuel its investment portfolio in the region's most populous country. The establishment of the UAE capital's new headquarters crowns the US$20 billion investment rostrum initiated in 2019 between the two countries' respective SWFs. This strategic partnership is expected to catalyze Egypt's economic growth and development, especially since that is intended to penetrate some SDG-related projects in the healthcare, food security, real estate, and financial sectors. Such collaboration provides evidence of the enormous growth potential enjoyed by Egypt and the promising business environment it has succeeded in marketing to external specialized funds and key investment tool-holders. Evidently, the IMF country outlook released in July 2021 showcased how Egypt presented itself as the only Middle East nation to actually deliver positive GDP growth rates amid the COVID-19 health crisis. The Egyptian government was also praised for its macroeconomic policy management, which was described as both agile and resilient in facing the outbreak (IMF, 2021).

The Fund's governance structure claims to be based on sound and universally called-for practices ratified by the IFSWF. Nevertheless, questions in regard to decision-making procedures emerged with the exclusive rights given to the latter upon asset acquisition, and this was further accompanied by decree immunizing such sales against public opinion and questioning. Other debatable issues revolve around the sole power granted to the president with respect to the selection and appointment of both the executive board and president.

The Fund's governance structure promises the provision of transparency and integrity guaranteed by its competent supervisory board of directors that was handpicked according to expertise. The fund's mandate asserts its fair representation in front of judicial inspection, should circumstances entail so, and hence is committed to accountability measures wherever necessary. The Fund is expected to go through record scrutiny by the Egyptian Central Audit Organization[46] where, according to Egyptian law, its annual reports are supposed to be submitted to the Fund's Board prior to the President and Parliament. According to Haroun (2021), audit controls are also executed by the Central Bank of Egypt (CBE) and Financial Regulatory Authority.

8.5 SWFs in India as an EM

Up to 2015, India was the only BRICS country that did not own a SWF. In 2015–2016, the then finance minister created the first strategic one, named the National Investment and Infrastructure Fund, or the NIIF. During the five years following that date, the Indian market managed to attract substantial investments from the Gulf region, particularly the state of Qatar, and specifically in the field of infrastructure. Considering the huge infrastructure requirements the country has, it comes with no surprise that this sector received the lion's share of FDIs from offshore locations. India also embarked on attempts to promote itself as a promising market for SWFs investments, where the government would sponsor and endorse partnerships with counter SWFs and the private sector.

As per the latest disclosed information, the NIIF[47] manages three sub-funds, each specialized in one particular sector as follows: (1) The Master Fund, which is an infra-related fund and focuses on developing infrastructure and procurement projects like roads, ports, and airports. (2) Funds of Funds – this fund

---

[46] The Central Audit Organization (CAO) is an independent body with a public legal persona affiliated with the president of the country, whose affairs are regulated by specific laws in the country's constitution. The CAO aims to achieve control over state funds, funds of other public entities, as well as persons stipulated in the law. The House of Representatives assists in carrying out its duties in this supervision. The CAO exercises control through the following forms: (1) Financial control, both accounting and legal. (2) Monitoring the performance and following up the implementation of the plan. Legal oversight of decisions issued in relation to financial violations.

[47] As per the data available on the NIIF website in January 2021, NIIF manages a corpus of US$4.4 billion across three sub-funds.

invests in the funds operated by fund managers and is specialized in social infrastructure projects such as affordable housing, education, and healthcare. (3) The Strategic Opportunities Investment Fund is actually a private equity investment fund and is active with equity investment instruments.

The Indian government possesses a 49 percent stake of ownership of the NIIF,[48] making it an unconventional SWF relative to its worldwide counterparts (Garg & Shukla, 2021b). In 2017, it managed to sign off a contract agreeing to partner with Abu Dhabi's Investment Authority (ADIA) with a sum reaching US$1 billion. Other well-known co-investments that have been recorded on the NIIF's official website include Temasek, Singapore, and the Asian Development Bank. Simultaneously, several offshore SWFs took interest in co-investing in India's capital markets. During the pandemic, and particularly in the last quarter of 2020, India was identified as the second most favored destination for SWFs' investments after the USA, according to the Global SWF data. Real estate, venture financing, and IPOs earned the most attraction.

Governance Framework

In early 2017, the NIIF ratified a one-of-a-kind governance element in the form of a policy called the whistleblowing policy. Ratified in 2020, the policy was an extension of a "code of conduct" that strives to fight corruption in all its forms, misuse of power, and ensure the presence of transparency and information disclosure to the best of all possible standards. According to records made available by the NIIF's official website, the whistleblowing policy and its code of conduct are meant to set the framework needed to deal with any reported cases of improper activity, illegal, and unethical conduct or misconduct that are proven factual. Such a framework seeks to ensure the welfare of all stakeholders involved with or deal directly with the Fund.

Investing in SDG Projects

The NIIF acts as an intercessor between the Indian government, Indian investors, International investors, as well as outbound SWFs. Substantial capital has poured into India's infrastructure sectors, yet growing interest has also been devoted to renewable energy, water and waste management. The Fund established its own Environment and Social Management Framework (ESMF), which addresses keys sustainable development elements such as (1) Environmental and Social (E&S) Management Policy, (2) E&S Management

---

[48] In short, the National Investment and Infrastructure Fund Limited (NIIFL) is a collaborative investment platform for international and Indian investors, anchored by the Government of India.

Principles, and (3) E&S Management Procedures and Guidelines. The ESMF policy sees that investments are in compliance with the country's national environment and social agendas and adhere to the regulations and policies of SDGs. The policy comprises four main principles, one of which relates to assessing the environmental impacts and risks of a particular investment, and explores ways of mitigating such risks. Such mitigation seeks to ensure the compliance with applicable environmental standards in an effort to maximize benefits to communities that rely on environmental resources exposed to any risk due to such investment.

Though characterized by low per capita income, India's economy is growing at an unprecedented rate. Relative to other EMs, India has shown robust growth in manufacturing, business-friendly reforms, infrastructural development, and political stability that makes the country one of the most prominent EMs to invest in. Up until 2015, India's foreign policies were not exactly the most encouraging ones to allure FDIs onto its soil. Yet, with remarkable reforms on that front, the country succeeded in reforming its outlook to FDIs and has been promoting itself as an attractive destination for offshore investors due to the agility and ease of doing business indicators it has worked on improving.

Future Prospects for EMs

It is true that EMs by nature bear higher risks relative to more-developed countries as they suffer from more uncertainty in their capital markets, more chances of inflation, and rising contractionary monetary measures, and are often believed to be more susceptible to economic downturns than others. Yet, EMs carry the potential to rapidly grow amid slowing economic performance – as shown during the pandemic of 2020 – and possess room for higher returns on investment. India in particular managed to offer the world a robust, diversified, and well-regulated financial system capable of welcoming influxes of foreign capital.

Conclusion

Regardless of the mandates SWFs choose to follow, there is no doubt they have proliferated considerably in the past decade. Their rise and dominance in EMs were of special emphasis in this Element. Whether recent discoveries of natural resources (e.g., Ghana), improvements in democratic regimes driven by economic structural reforms (Egypt and India), and/or world crises that catalyzed their growth, there is no doubt they now dominate the future landscapes of their state owners. They currently occupy a prominent role in facilitating capital flows across international financial markets and are promising the world to harness their investments toward achieving the SDGs. Accordingly, multiple governance assessment instruments were devised to quantify their degrees of transparency, resilience to disruptors, and commitment to sustainability. Evidence has shown that the higher they scored across these categories, the more they attracted capital investments from interested partners from different sectors. EMs played both parts in this scene – as investors and hosts. As investors, their SWFs, especially those captured in this study, lagged behind their western counterparts in governance indicators despite some apparent improvements in the past few years.[49] Nevertheless, their healthy appetites toward diversification and sustainability (as in the case of KSA, UAE, and Egypt) mitigated such challenges and have allowed for more and more collaborations with private-sector partners and sister SWFs across borders (in the case of Egypt and India).

As recipients, EMs staged a fertile ecosystem for guest SWFs. In the examples explored in this Element, some of them mastered the art of opening their markets to all serious foreign investors and worked hard to provide the facilitating regulatory framework to do so, as in the case of UAE and India. Others have developed unique AUM setups to convince international capital owners of their legitimacy and capacity to collaborate (as in the case of Egypt and Ghana), promising to utilize their abundant reservoirs of human and natural resources to close their deals. All examples discussed here promised to decouple their economic objectives from any political orientation that could raise red flags at their investment strategies. Although difficult to do so, the fact that the larger percentage of partners resides in the private sector, tends to ratify such claims.

In all cases, and despite the long way they are still to take, SWFs in EMs are more trusted than five or ten years ago. They have come a long way to reach the positions they now occupy and could still do more in terms of their data sharing and transparency.

Policy Recommendations

At the time of writing this Element, worldwide events – which were of no focal point in this study – drove oil prices up like never before in the past few years.[50]

---

[49] Namely, Australia's Future Fund, Norway's NBIM (Norges Bank Investment Management), and New Zealand's Super Fund.

[50] At the time of writing this Element, the world was barely recovering from the COVID-19 pandemic, only to be struck by a war in the eastern European hemisphere between Russia and Ukraine. Although the war is of no strong relevance in this study, it had profound impact on the prices of oil, natural gas, and the supplies of some strategic food products. These price fluctuations, along with those traced in financial markets, will shape the way ahead for SWFs in terms of their investment decisions.

Although this may come as good news for commodity-based SWFs that rely heavily on oil revenues, it may act as a setback for responsible investing initiatives. Accordingly, concerned SOEs (KSA & UAE) are advised to continue funding their ESG-based projects from their diversified investment portfolios while continuing to decarbonize their investment baskets. Moreover, there is no better timing for them to begin disclosing their climate targets, given how their economies' longstanding reliance on fossil fuels. Despite recognized efforts to boost ESG focus across the named countries, a tougher challenge now emerges to commit to responsible investing even more than any other time. This recommendation is endorsed by the fact that evidence has proven a repulsion in investors' capital from SWFs/private-sector companies with poor ESG ratings. Unfortunately, despite a rise in annual investments in renewables, IFSWF analytics point out how oil and gas deals in 2021 still surpass renewable ones. While oil and gas investment earnings are more lucrative, they could actually assist their commodity-based sovereign funds transition away from carbon-heavy projects into more sustainable ones. A second recommendation falls in the realm of clearly understanding the challenges SWFs face, especially those of medium- to small-size AUM. It is true that SWFs offer substantial opportunities for sustainable development in their home countries, yet they should always be regarded as one tool out of an array of many others to do the job. Policymakers need to accurately estimate the potential impact their SWFs carry rather than overestimating them, believing they could attend to all development challenges. In the case of Egypt, for example, it is crucial that its SWF is directed to complement a more comprehensive set of macroeconomic policies meant to better utilize available resource endowments. It may not be feasible to fully embed it into the national budget as such, but aligning it to the promising structural reforms already in place will render better outcomes. It is critical for state owners to employ SWFs as supplementary fiscal tools and acknowledge them as pieces of a larger resource-management strategy.

Having said that, Egypt's "wealth-less" SWF is actually a success story that could be portrayed as a viable business model for countries with similar economic profiles. TSFE succeeded in expediting public–private partnerships and FDIs, and its footsteps could be followed by its counterparts. Nevertheless, lessons learned from the Egyptian case will only be amplified if considerable effort is put to improve public disclosure practices, governance, and transparency.

References

Al-Hassan, A., Papaioannou, M. M. G., Skancke, M., & Sung, C. C. (2013). *Sovereign wealth funds: Aspects of governance structures and investment management*. International Monetary Fund.

Alsweilem, K. A., Cummine, A., Rietveld, M., & Tweedie, K. (2015). *Sovereign investor models: Institutions and policies for managing sovereign wealth*. John F. Kennedy School of Government, Center for Science and International Affairs and Center for International Development, Harvard Kennedy School. www.ifswf.org/sites/default/files/Publications/InvestorModels.pdf. Accessed September 26, 2021.

Amihud, Y., Hameed, A., Kang, W., & Zhang, H. (2015). The illiquidity premium: International evidence. *Journal of Financial Economics*, *117*(2), 350–368.

Arinze-Umobi, C., & Ihedirionye, C. C. (2021). African sovereign wealth funds and government influence: A clog in the wheel of economic development. *International Journal of Comparative Law and Legal Philosophy (IJOCLLEP)*, *3*(2).

Arouri, M., Boubaker, S., & Grais, W. (2018). On the determinants of sovereign wealth funds' investments: Are Arab SWFs different? *Economic Research Forum Working Paper* (No. 1174). https://erf.org.cg/app/uploads/2018/03/1174Final.pdf.Accessed September 1, 2021.

Bassan, F., ed. (2015). *Research handbook on sovereign wealth funds and international investment law*. Edward Elgar.

Bauer, A., & Mihalyi, D. (2018). Premature funds: How overenthusiasm and bad advice can leave countries poorer. *Natural Resource Governance Institute Briefing*. https://resourcegovernance.org/sites/default/files/documents/premature-funds. Accessed September 1, 2021.

Beuermann, D., Schwartz, M., Reyes-Tagle, G., et al. (2021). *Economic institutions for a resilient Caribbean*. IDB Publications (Books).

Blundell-Wignall, A., Hu, Y. W., & Yermo, J. (2008). Sovereign wealth and pension fund issues. *OECD Working Papers on Insurance and Private Pensions* (No. 14). https://doi.org/10.1787/243287223503.

Bortolotti, B., Fotak, V., & Megginson, W. L. B. (2015). The rise of sovereign wealth funds: Definition, organization, and governance. In S. Caselli, G. Corbetta, & V. Vecchi (eds.), *Public private partnerships for infrastructure and business development* (pp. 295–318). Palgrave Macmillan.

Boubakri, N., Cosset, J. C., & Grira, J. (2016). Sovereign wealth funds targets selection: A comparison with pension funds. *Journal of International Financial Markets, Institutions and Money, 42*, 60–76.

Braunstein, J. (2017). Sovereign wealth funds: The catalyst for climate finance. *World Bank.* https://blogs.worldbank.org/psd/sovereign-wealth-funds-catalyst-climate-finance. Accessed August 26, 2021.

Carney, R. W. (2021). Sovereign wealth funds' investment purpose and the investment implications. https://papers.ssrn.com/sol3/papers.cfm?abstract_id=3902962. Accessed September 1, 2021.

Center for the Governance of Change. (2019). Sovereign wealth funds 2019. https://docs.ie.edu/cgc/research/sovereign-wealth/SOVEREIGN-WEALTH-RESEARCH-IE-CGC-REPORT_2019.pdf. Accessed August 1, 2021.

Cevik, M. S., & Jalles, J. T. (2020). *This changes everything: Climate shocks and sovereign bonds.* International Monetary Fund.

Chen, J. (2019). Financing the sustainable development goals: The role of African sovereign wealth funds. *New York University Journal of International Law and Politics, 51*, 1259.

Clark, G. L., Dixon, A. D., & Monk, A. H. (2013). *Sovereign wealth funds.* Princeton University Press.

Cumming, D. J., Wood, G., Filatotchev, I., & Reinecke, J., eds. (2017). *The Oxford handbook of sovereign wealth funds.* Oxford University Press.

Das, D. K. (2009). Sovereign-wealth funds: The institutional dimension. *International Review of Economics, 56*(1), 85–104.

Dixon, A. D. (2013). Enhancing the transparency dialogue in the Santiago Principles for sovereign wealth funds. *Seattle University Law Review, 37*, 581.

Duttagupta, R., & Pazarbasioglu, C. (2021). MILESto go. *Finance & Development, International Monetary Fund.* www.imf.org/external/pubs/ft/fandd/2021/06/pdf/the-future-of-emerging-markets-duttagupta-and-pazar-basioglu.pdf. Accessed September 8, 2021.

Elbadawi, I., Soto, R., & Zaki, C. (2018). Sovereign wealth funds, cross-border investment bias and institutions: The case of Arab countries. *Economic Research Forum Working Paper* (No. 1173).

Elbadawi, I., Soto, R., & Zaki, C. (2020). Sovereign wealth funds and cross-border investment bias: The case of Arab countries. *Middle East Development Journal,* 12(1), 1–23.

Elbaz, O. (2018). The role of sovereign funds in promoting external stability of the home economy. *Scholedge International Journal of Management & Development ISSN 2394–3378, 5*(9), 96–113. https://thescholedge.org/index.php/sijmd/article/view/499. Accessed September 8, 2021.

Engel, J., Barbary, V., Hamirani, H., & Saklatvala, K. (2020). Sovereign wealth funds and innovation investing in an era of mounting uncertainty. *World Intellectual Property Organization*. www.wipo.int/edocs/pubdocs/en/wipo_pub_gii_2020-chapter5.pdf. Accessed November 29, 2021.

Evenett, S. J. (2019). Protectionism, state discrimination, and international business since the onset of the global financial crisis. *Journal of International Business Policy, 2*(1), 9–36.

Fratto, C., Vannier, B. H., Mircheva, M., de Padua, D., & Ward, M. H. P. (2021). *Unconventional monetary policies in emerging markets and frontier countries.* International Monetary Fund.

Garg, R., & Shukla, A. (2021a). The impact and implications of SWFs: A systematic review of literature. *Qualitative Research in Financial Markets, 13*(5), 580–607. https://doi.org/10.1108/QRFM-08-2020-0171.

Garg, R., & Shukla, A. (2021b). Sovereign wealth funds: A critical analysis. *Business Analyst, 41*(2), 25–47.

Ghosh, I. (2019). Transforming emerging economies with sovereign development funds. *World Economic Forum*. www.weforum.org/agenda/2019/02/trans forming-emergingeconomies-with-sovereign-development-funds/. Accessed August 24, 2021.

Global SWF. (2022). Largest sovereign wealth funds worldwide as of January 2022, by assets under management. www.statista.com/statistics/276617/sov ereign-wealth-funds-worldwide-based-on-assets-under-management. Accessed April 12, 2022.

Griffith-Jones, S., & Ocampo, J. A. (2011). The rationale for sovereign wealth funds from a development perspective. In J. Stiglitz, P. Bolton, & F. Samama (eds.), *Sovereign wealth funds and long-term investing* (pp. 60–66). Columbia University Press.

Grira, J. (2020). Back to government ownership: The sovereign wealth funds phenomenon. *Finance Research Letters, 34*, 101245.

Gupta, J., Rempel, A., & Verrest, H. (2020). Access and allocation: The role of large shareholders and investors in leaving fossil fuels underground. *International Environmental Agreements: Politics, Law and Economics, 20* (2), 303–322.

Haroun, M. (2021). Analysis of managing and transferring of ownership of public land assests in Egypt: TSFE "The Sovereign Fund of Egypt". Second Arab Land Conference, February 22–24, Cairo, Egypt. https://arabstates.gltn .net/wp-content/uploads/2021/03/TechnicalSession2_TSFE_Ismael_AUC-pre sentation.pdf. Accessed October 13, 2021.

Hentov, E., & Petrov, A. (2015). How do sovereign wealth funds invest: A glance at SWF asset allocation. www.ifswf.org/sites/default/files/Publications/

How %20do%20Sovereign%20Wealth%20Funds%20Invest_0.pdf. Accessed September 2, 2021.

Hentov, E., & Petrov, A. (2017). How do sovereign investors approach ESG investing? *State Street Global Advisors*. www.ssga.com/content/dam/SSGA/pdfs/investment-topics/environmental-social-governance/2017/How-Do-Sovereign-Investors-Approach-ESG-Investing.pdf. Accessed September 1, 2021.

IFSWF. (2020a). The Egypt fund becomes an associate member of the IFSWF. www.ifswf.org/general-news/egypt-fund-becomes-associate-member-ifswf. Accessed December 22, 2021.

IFSWF. (2020b). Mighty oaks from little acorns grow: Sovereign wealth funds' progress on climate change. www.ifswf.org/sites/default/files/IFSWF_Climate_Change_Feb2020%20FINAL.pdf. Accessed September 5, 2021.

IFSWF. (2021a). Investing for growth and prosperity: In Africa sovereign wealth funds focus on G, S and E. www.ifswf.org/sites/default/files/IFSWF_Africa_Paper_v2.pdf. Accessed December 3, 2021.

IFSWF. (2021b). LMTI: Middle Eastern sovereign funds reduce reporting transparency. www.swfinstitute.org/news/85520/lmti-middle-eastern-sovereign-funds-reduce-reporting-transparency. Accessed April 12, 2022.

IFSWF. (2021c). Santiago Principles' for clarity and alter the citation accordingly? www.ifswf.org/santiago-principles. Accessed July 28, 2021.

IFSWF. (2021d). State-owned investors in a post-pandemic age. https://global-swf.s3.amazonaws.com/file-uploads/ibdoIlDQ1fH8ckTg00BTZfqJNZRw6jdVHCbLLKMm.pdf. Accessed March 3, 2022.

IMF. (2007). "Market Developments and Issues." Financial Stability Report, April 2007. www.imf.org/en/publications/gfsr.

IMF. (2021). Arab Republic of Egypt: 2021 Article IV consultation, second review under the stand-by arrangement-press release; staff report; and statement by the executive Director for the Arab Republic of Egypt. *ISBN: 9781513592046/1934 7685*. www.imf.org/en/Publications/CR/Issues/2021/07/22/Arab-Republic-of-Egypt-2021-Article-IV-Consultation-Second-Review-Under-the-Stand-By-462545. •

Kalter, E., & Schena, P. (2013). Into the institutional void: Managing sovereign wealth of emerging economies. In D. Cumming, G. Wood, I. Filatotchev, & J. Reinecke (eds.), *Investing in emerging and frontier markets* (pp. 17–34). Euromoney Books.

Kotter, J., & Lel, U. (2011). Friends or foes? Target selection decisions of sovereign wealth funds and their consequences. *Journal of Financial Economics*, *101*(2), 360–381.

Lessambo, F. I. (2021). International finance. In *International finance* (pp. 1–5). Palgrave Macmillan.

Liang, H., & Renneboog, L. (2020). The global sustainability footprint of sovereign wealth funds. *Oxford Review of Economic Policy*, *36*(2), 380–426.

Liu, I., & Dixon, A. (2019). The Santiago Principles 2.0: Advancing the agenda. *IFSWF*. https://archive.ifswfreview.org/2018/our-partners/santiago-princip les-20-advancing-agenda. Accessed October 1, 2021.

Liu, P., Mauck, N., & Price, S. M. (2020). Are government owned investment funds created equal? Evidence from sovereign wealth fund real estate acquisitions. *The Journal of Real Estate Finance and Economics*, *61*(4), 698–729.

Lorfing, P. A. (2021). Screening of foreign direct investment and the states' security interests in light of the OECD, UNCTAD and other international guidelines. *Public Actors in International Investment Law*, 179–199. https:// doi.org/10.1007%2F978-3-030-58916-5_10.

Maire, J., Mazarei, A., & Truman, E. M. (2021a). Sovereign wealth funds are growing more slowly, and governance issues remain. *Peterson Institute for International Economics Working Paper* (No. PB21-3). www.piie.com/publi cations/policy-briefs/sovereign-wealth-funds-are-growing-more-slowly-and -governance-issues. Accessed October 1, 2021.

Maire, J., Mazarei, A., & Truman, E. M. (2021b). Uncertain Prospects for Sovereign Wealth Funds of Gulf Countries. *Peterson Institute for International Economics Working Paper* (No. PB21-4). www.piie.com /sites/default/files/documents/pb21-4.pdf. Accessed December 17, 2021.

Markowitz, C. (2020). Sovereign wealth funds in Africa: Taking stock and looking forward. *South African Institute of International Affairs*. https:// media.africaportal.org/documents/Occasional-Paper-304-markowitz.pdf. Accessed September 26, 2022.

McPherson-Smith, O. (2021). Diversification, Khashoggi, and Saudi Arabia's public investment fund. *Global Policy*, *12*(2), 190–203.

Megginson, W. L., Lopez, D., & Malik, A. (2020). The rise of state-owned investors: Sovereign wealth funds and public pension funds. *Annual Review of Financial Economics*, *13*(1), 247–270.

Meng, C. (2020). Sovereign wealth funds as international institutional investors 1: A re-evaluation. In L. Bernier, M. Florio, & P. Bance (eds.), *The Routledge handbook of state-owned enterprises* (pp. 372–389). Routledge. https://doi .org/10.4324/9781351042543.

Ministry of Finance, Ghana. (2017). Ghana investment infrastructure fund: Investment policy statement. www.mofep.gov.gh/sites/default/files/reports/ economic/GIIF%20Investment%20Policy%20Statement_April62017.pdf. Accessed December 4, 2021.

Mody, A. (2003). What is an emerging market? *International Monetary Fund.* www.imf.org/en/Publications/WP/Issues/2016/12/31/What-is-An-Emerging -Market-17598. Accessed September 8, 2021.

Mulder M., Das, U., Lu, Y., Mulder, C., & Sy, A. N. R. (2009). Setting up a sovereign wealth fund: Some policy and operational considerations. *International Monetary Fund*, 9–179.

Murtinu, S., & Scalera, V. G. (2016). Sovereign wealth funds' internationalization strategies: The use of investment vehicles. *Journal of International Management, 22*(3), 249–264.

OECD. (2020). COVID-19 crisis threatens sustainable development goals financing. www.oecd.org/newsroom/covid-19-crisis-threatens-sustainable-development-goals-financing.htm#:~:text=10%2F11%2F2020%20%2D%20 According,as%20governments%20and%20investors%20grapple. Accessed July 21 2021.

OECD. (2021). Mobilising institutional investors for financing sustainable development in developing countries: Emerging evidence of opportunities and challenges. www.oecd.org/officialdocuments/publicdisplaydocumentpdf/? cote=DCD(2021)11&docLanguage=En. Accessed August 26, 2021.

Onifade, T. T. (2016). *Regulating Natural Resource Funds* (Master's thesis, Graduate Studies).

OPSWF. (2018). One planet sovereign wealth funds framework. https://onepla netswfs.org/wp-content/pdfjs/web/viewer.html?file=https://oneplanetswfs .org/download/23/online-publication/550/oneplanetswf_online.pdf. Accessed September 3, 2021.

Ouni, Z., Bernard, P., & Plaisent, M. (2020). Sovereign wealth funds definition: Challenges and concerns. *Advances in Economics and Business, 8*(6), 362–376. https://doi.org/10.13189/AEB.2020.080605.

PwC. (2020). Sovereign Investors 2020: A growing force. www.pwc.com/gx/en/ sovereign-wealth-investment-funds/publications/assets/sovereign-investors -2020.pdf. Accessed September 17, 2021.

Sharma, R. (2017). *Sovereign wealth funds investment in sustainable development sectors*. Global Projects Center, Stanford University.

Sidra Capital. (2021). Sovereign wealth funds in the aftermath of the COVID-19 crisis. https://sidracapital.com/wp-content/uploads/2021/08/Sovereign-Wealth-Funds_21-June-202162.pdf. Accessed December 17, 2021.

Sovereign Wealth Fund Institute. (2008). What is a sovereign wealth fund. www.swfinstitute.org/research/sovereign-wealth-fund. Accessed July 26, 2021.

Staista. (2021). Largest sovereign wealth funds worldwide as of December 2021, by assets under management. www.statista.com/statistics/276617/sover

eign-wealth-funds-worldwide-based-on-assets-under-management. Accessed September 8, 2021.

Stocker, M., Baffes, J., Some, Y. M., Vorisek, D., & Wheeler, C. M. (2018). The 2014–16 oil price collapse in retrospect: Sources and implications. *World Bank Policy Research Working Paper* (No. 8419).

Stone, S. E., & Truman, E. M. (2016). Uneven progress on sovereign wealth fund transparency and accountability. *Peterson Institute for International Economics Working Paper* (No. PB16-18). www.piie.com/system/files/docu ments/pb16-18.pdf. Accessed September 1, 2021.

Triki, T., & Faye, I. (2011). Africa's quest for development: Can sovereign wealth funds help? In N. Boubakri & J.-C. Cosset (eds.), *Institutional invest- ors in global capital markets* (pp. 263–290). Emerald Group.

Truman, E. M. (2011). Sovereign wealth funds: Is Asia different? *Peterson Institute for International Economics Working Paper* (No. 11–12).

Tsani, S., & Overland, I. (2020). Sovereign wealth funds and public financing for climate action. In W. Leal Filho, A. Azul, L. Brandli, P. Ozuyar, & T. Wall (eds.), *Climate action*. Encyclopedia of the UN Sustainable Development Goals (pp. 130–131). Springer. https://doi.org/10.1007/978-3-319-95885-9.

UNCTAD. (2014). World Investment Report 2014: Investing in the SDGs: An action plan. https://unctad.org/system/files/official-document/wir2014_en .pdf. Accessed August 1, 2021.

UNCTAD. (2020). How public pension and sovereign wealth funds mainstream sustainability. https://unctad.org/system/files/official-document/diae2020 d3_en.pdf. Accessed August 22, 2021.

UNCTAD. (2021). World Investment Report 2021: Investing in sustainable recovery. https://unctad.org/system/files/official-document/wir2021_en.pdf. Accessed July 30, 2021.

Virgis, A. (2020). Sustainable business models and B corps: Exploring impact performance in an international setting. https://thesis.unipd.it/bitstream/20 .500.12608/21048/1/Virgis_Alice.pdf. Accessed on October 30, 2022.

Wafi, O. (2021). Quick moves of the sovereign fund of Egypt. *Center for International and Strategic Studies*. https://synerjies.com/quick-moves-of- the-sovereign-fund-of-egypt. Accessed December 23, 2021.

Wang, D., & Li, Q. (2016). Democracy, veto player, and institutionalization of sovereign wealth funds. *International Interactions*, *42*(3), 377–400.

Wills, S. (2018). Leave the volatility fund alone: Principles for managing oil wealth. *Journal of Macroeconomics*, *55*, 332–352.

World Economic Forum. (2018). Thinking strategically: Using resource revenues to invest in a sustainable future. www3.weforum.org/docs/WEF_Thin king_Strategically.pdf. Accessed September 27, 2021.

Wurster, S., & Schlosser, S. J. (2021). Sovereign wealth funds as sustainability instruments? Disclosure of sustainability criteria in worldwide comparison. *Sustainability*, *13*(10), 5565.

Young, K. E. (2020). Sovereign risk: Gulf sovereign wealth funds as engines of growth and political resource. *British Journal of Middle Eastern Studies*, *47*(1), 96–116.

Yu, C., & Yang, L. (2017). Implications of sovereign wealth funds on the governance of the middle East region. *Asian Journal of Middle Eastern and Islamic Studies*, *11*(4), 64–75.

Zhan, J. X., & Santos-Paulino, A. U. (2021). Investing in the sustainable development goals: Mobilization, channeling, and impact. *Journal of International Business Policy*, *4*(1), 166–183.

Cambridge Elements ≡

Economics of Emerging Markets

Bruno S. Sergi
Harvard University

Editor Bruno S. Sergi is an Instructor at Harvard University, an Associate of the Harvard University Davis Center for Russian and Eurasian Studies and Harvard Ukrainian Research Institute. He is the Academic Series Editor of the Cambridge *Elements in the Economics of Emerging Markets* (Cambridge University Press), a co-editor of the *Lab for Entrepreneurship and Development* book series, and associate editor of *The American Economist*. Concurrently, he teaches International Economics at the University of Messina, Scientific Director of the Lab for Entrepreneurship and Development (LEAD), and a co-founder and Scientific Director of the International Center for Emerging Markets Research at RUDN University in Moscow. He has published over 150 articles in professional journals and twenty-one books as author, co-author, editor, and co-editor.

About the Series

The aim of this Elements series is to deliver state-of-the-art, comprehensive coverage of the knowledge developed to date, including the dynamics and prospects of these economies, focusing on emerging markets' economics, finance, banking, technology advances, trade, demographic challenges, and their economic relations with the rest of the world, as well as the causal factors and limits of economic policy in these markets.

Cambridge Elements

Economics of Emerging Markets

A full series listing is available at: www.cambridge.org/EEM